What's the Best Television Trivia Book?

1,600 Questions Across 7 Decades

David Fickes

Introduction

By nature, I tend to collect trivia without trying. Until relatively recently, I had never sought out trivia; however, after creating a holiday trivia presentation for a community party and then showing it at one of our fitness studio spinning classes, I found myself creating weekly trivia. The cycling clients enjoyed the diversion of answering questions while they exercised, so I continued.

What you find in most trivia is a lot of erroneous or outdated information or questions that are so simple or esoteric that they aren't interesting. It is difficult to come up with interesting questions that are at the right level of difficulty that a wide variety of people can enjoy them, and they are something that you feel you should know or want to know. I have tried to ensure that the information is as accurate as possible, and to retain its accuracy, I have also tried to avoid questions whose answers can easily change with time.

Television trivia is fun because it brings back so many memories; you can often see the answers visually in your mind. There are 1,600 questions in 8 categories arranged by decades from the 1950s to the 2010s plus an all-time category. Shows are categorized by the decade they first aired. To make it quick and easy to test yourself or others without initially seeing the answers, each category is divided into short quizzes with 10 questions followed by their answers.

This is book 4 of my *What's the Best Trivia?* series; I hope you enjoy it, and if you do, look for other books in the series covering a variety of trivia topics.

Contents

All-Time

Quiz 1

1) Who was the first woman to host *Saturday Night Live*?
2) Who was the first U.S. president to hold a televised news conference?
3) Who is the oldest person to host *Saturday Night Live*?
4) What was the first streaming series to win the Outstanding Comedy Series Emmy?
5) Who was the original host of *The Tonight Show*?
6) What year was cigarette advertising banned from U.S. television?
7) What is the longest running game show in the U.S.?
8) Who was the first woman to run a major television studio?
9) What major cable network put on a polka festival as its first attempt at original programming?
10) Who was the first person to win Emmys for acting, writing, and directing for the same series?

Quiz 1 Answers

1) Candace Bergen – 1975
2) Dwight D. Eisenhower
3) Betty White – 88
4) *The Marvelous Mrs. Maisel* (2018) – Amazon
5) Steve Allen
6) 1971
7) *The Price is Right* – started in 1972
8) Lucille Ball – She ran Desilu Studio starting in 1962; the studio produced many popular shows including *Mission Impossible* and *Star Trek*.
9) HBO
10) Alan Alda – *M*A*S*H*

Quiz 2

1) What was the first feature film broadcast on U.S. television?
2) What is the Cookie Monster's real name on *Sesame Street*?
3) Prior to *Law & Order* in the 1990s, what was the longest running

U.S. crime show?
4) What year were the first Olympics broadcast in the U.S.?
5) What year did *Saturday Night Live* debut?
6) What was the first toy advertised on U.S. television?
7) Who was the first automaker to advertise on network television?
8) What series has the most watched episode in U.S. television history?
9) What sitcom marked the acting debut of Jerry Seinfeld?
10) What was the last television series produced by Lucille Ball's production company Desilu?

Quiz 2 Answers

1) *The Wizard of Oz* – broadcast in 1956
2) Sid
3) *Hawaii Five-O* (1968–1980)
4) 1960 – Squaw Valley, California Winter Olympics
5) 1975
6) Mr. Potato Head – 1952
7) Chevrolet – 1946
8) *M*A*S*H* – series finale in 1983 with over 105 million viewers
9) *Benson* – 1980
10) *Mannix* (1967–1975)

Quiz 3

1) What year was the first NFL game televised?
2) In what year did the first television couple share a bed?
3) What U.S. show featured the first openly gay character?
4) What year did Nielsen start providing television ratings data?
5) What is the longest running animated children's show in the U.S.?
6) What was the first American series to feature teenagers as the lead characters?
7) Who played Captain Kangaroo?
8) In its 2002 list of the 50 greatest television shows of all time, *TV Guide* listed two animated shows, what were they?
9) What year was the World Series broadcast live for the first time?
10) What sportscaster was the host of *ABC's Wide World of Sports*?

Quiz 3 Answers

1) 1939
2) 1947 – on *Mary Kay and Johnny* which was the first sitcom ever
3) *Soap* – 1977
4) 1950
5) *Arthur* – It started on PBS in 1996.
6) *The Many Loves of Dobie Gillis* – 1959
7) Bob Keeshan
8) *The Simpsons* and *Rocky and Bullwinkle*
9) 1947
10) Jim McKay

Quiz 4

1) The character of Sheriff Andy Taylor first appeared on what show?
2) What show featured the first interracial kiss broadcast in the U.S.?
3) What year did *Sesame Street* debut?
4) What series at its height aired in 148 countries on every inhabited continent and was once called the most watched television show in the world by *The Guinness Book of World Records*?
5) What is the only primetime drama to be spun off from two separate shows?
6) What year did U.S. commercial networks first broadcast a majority of their primetime shows in color?
7) What was the first American sitcom to film in Russia?
8) Who made the Rolling Stones sing "Let's spend the night together" as "Let's spend some time together"?
9) What actress has played the same role for the longest time on U.S. live action primetime television?
10) On what sitcom did Frank Sinatra make his final television appearance?

Quiz 4 Answers

1) *The Danny Thomas Show* – later spun off to *The Andy Griffith Show*
2) *Star Trek* – Uhura and Captain Kirk kissed in 1968.
3) 1969
4) *Baywatch* (1989-2001)

5) *Law & Order: Special Victims Unit* - It spun off from *Law & Order* (1990) and the character of Detective John Munch came from *Homicide: Life on the Street* (1993-1999).
6) 1965
7) *Head of the Class* (1986-1991)
8) Ed Sullivan
9) Mariska Hargitay - She has played Olivia Benson on *Law & Order: Special Victims Unit* since 1999.
10) *Who's the Boss*

Quiz 5

1) What year was the first televised presidential debate?
2) What was the first hour long western on U.S. television?
3) What year did *American Bandstand* debut?
4) What was the first game show broadcast on commercial television?
5) What year did the reality show *Survivor* debut?
6) What is the longest running morning show in the U.S.?
7) What two series are tied for the most consecutive Outstanding Comedy Series Emmys at five?
8) What show has a Guinness World Record for most swearing in an animated series?
9) What was the first western to have all its episodes broadcast in color?
10) What is the longest running Superman series?

Quiz 5 Answers

1) 1960 - John F. Kennedy and Richard Nixon
2) *Cheyenne* (1955-1963)
3) 1952
4) *Truth or Consequences* – 1941
5) 2000
6) *Today* – started in 1952
7) *Frasier* (1994-1998) and *Modern Family* (2010-2014)
8) *South Park*
9) *Bonanza* (1959-1973)
10) *Smallville* (2001-2011)

Quiz 6

1) What was the first sitcom where the theme song was sung by the leading actors?
2) Donald Glover became only the second African American to win the Outstanding Lead Actor in a Comedy Series Emmy for what show?
3) What year did the reality show *The Bachelor* debut?
4) What is the longest running fitness show in the U.S.?
5) What year did Davy Crockett debut as a five-part *Disneyland* show?
6) For what series did John Ritter receive a posthumous Emmy nomination?
7) What year did the BBC start regular public television broadcasting in the United Kingdom?
8) What U.S. show had the first primetime toilet heard flushing?
9) Who was the original host of *Jeopardy!*?
10) What dramatic series had the first romantic kiss between two women on primetime U.S. television?

Quiz 6 Answers

1) *Green Acres* - Eddie Albert and Eva Gabor
2) *Atlanta* (2017)
3) 2002
4) *Gilad's Bodies in Motion* - 1983 to 2015
5) 1954
6) *8 Simple Rules* - Ritter died in September 2003 after the first season; the show continued in his absence.
7) 1932
8) *All in the Family* – 1971
9) Art Fleming – 1964 to 1984
10) *L.A. Law* - In 1991, female characters Abby played by Michele Greene and C.J. played by Amanda Donohoe kissed.

Quiz 7

1) What was the first weekly U.S. television series budgeted at over $1 million per episode?
2) What show had the first theme song to hit number one on Billboard's Hot 100?
3) What was the first television series filmed in color?
4) What is the oldest network newscast in the U.S.?

5) What year did *Gunsmoke* debut?
6) What was the first one-hour drama series produced by HBO?
7) What was the first show ever to air on Fox primetime?
8) What was the first series filmed before a live audience?
9) What two male dramatic characters appeared for the most consecutive years in U.S. live action primetime television?
10) What was the first cable series to win the Outstanding Drama Series Emmy?

Quiz 7 Answers

1) *Battlestar Galactica* - 1978
2) *S.W.A.T.* (1976) - "The Theme from S.W.A.T"
3) *The Cisco Kid* (1950-1956) - It was filmed in color from its first season, but its broadcasts were still black and white at the time.
4) *CBS Evening News* - started in 1948
5) 1955
6) *Oz* (1997-2003)
7) *Married with Children* - April 15, 1987
8) *I Love Lucy* - 1951
9) Matt Dillon played by James Arness on *Gunsmoke* from 1955 to 1975 and Detective John Munch played by Richard Belzer on *Homicide: Life on the Street* from 1993 to 1999 and on *Law & Order: Special Victims Unit* from 1999 to 2013
10) *The Sopranos* - 2006

Quiz 8

1) What was the first cable series to receive an Emmy nomination for Best Comedy Series?
2) What was the first U.S. network show to use the "F" word?
3) What show originated the term "jumped the shark" for when a show begins a decline in quality that it can't recover from?
4) What year was a television first installed at the British Prime Minister's residence at 10 Downing Street, London?
5) What was the first show to earn Emmys for all its principal cast members?
6) What long running science fiction show first aired in November 1963??
7) What was the first U.S. daily soap opera offered in syndication?
8) What was the first South American country with television?

9) What U.S. president had the first televised State of the Union Address?
10) What was the first U.S. primetime soap opera?

Quiz 8 Answers

1) *The Larry Sanders Show* – 1993
2) *Saturday Night Live*
3) *Happy Days* – During the season five opener, Fonzie jumped a shark while water skiing which marked the beginning of a sharp decline in the show's quality.
4) 1930 – Prime Minister Ramsay MacDonald and his family watched the first television drama ever on it.
5) *All in the Family*
6) *Doctor Who*
7) *Dark Shadows* (1966–1971)
8) Brazil – 1950
9) Harry Truman – 1947
10) *Peyton Place* (1964–1969)

Quiz 9

1) How tall is Big Bird on *Sesame Street*?
2) What is the longest running television show of any kind in the U.S.?
3) Who was Johnny Carson's final guest on *The Tonight Show*?
4) What are the only four U.S. television shows that were an hour long and had a laugh track?
5) Who is the first woman to win comedy acting Emmys for three different roles?
6) What was the last U.S. show to have its entire run filmed in black and white?
7) What was the first animated series to run in U.S. primetime?
8) Benjamin Kubelsky gained fame as what comedian?
9) Which of the *Law & Order* franchise series starts out showing the crime from the criminal's point of view?
10) What U.S. show has aired the most episodes ever?

Quiz 9 Answers

1) 8 feet 2 inches
2) *Meet the Press* – started in 1947

3) Bette Midler
4) *The Lucy-Desi Comedy Hour* (1957), *Love, American Style* (1969), *Eight is Enough* (1977), *The Love Boat* (1977)
5) Julia Louis-Dreyfus – *Seinfeld, The New Adventures of Old Christine, Veep*
6) *The Dick Van Dyke Show* – 1961 to 1966
7) *The Flintstones* – 1960
8) Jack Benny
9) *Law & Order: Criminal Intent* (2001-2011)
10) *SportsCenter* – over 50,000 unique episodes since 1979

Quiz 10

1) Who is regarded as the first television entertainer to step out of character and break the fourth wall by talking directly to the television audience?
2) U.S. television allows alcohol to be advertised if what?
3) Who was the first detective character that was created specifically for television and had not appeared in any other media?
4) What year did the U.S. begin transitioning to color television?
5) What U.S. live action sitcom character appeared for the most consecutive years?
6) What was the first show to end while it was still at the top of the Nielsen Ratings?
7) What classic U.S. sitcom was based on the British show *Till Death Us Do Part*?
8) Who was the first celebrity to make a guest appearance on *Sesame Street*?
9) Richard Anderson and Martin E. Brooks were the first actors in U.S. television history to play the same characters on two different series on two different networks at the same time; what were the two series they were on concurrently?
10) What was the first U.S. dramatic series to feature an African American actor in a lead role.

Quiz 10 Answers

1) George Burns – *The George Burns and Gracie Allen Show* (1950-1958)
2) As long as no alcohol is consumed in the commercial – It isn't a law or FCC regulation, just a broadcasting standard.
3) Peter Gunn – 1958

4) 1953
5) Frasier Crane - Between *Cheers* and *Frasier*, Kelsey Grammer played the character for 20 consecutive years.
6) *I Love Lucy*
7) *All in the Family*
8) James Earl Jones – He appeared on the show's second episode.
9) *The Six Million Dollar Man* and *The Bionic Woman* - They played Oscar Goldman and Dr. Rudy Wells on both shows which were originally both on ABC. *The Bionic Woman* moved to NBC in 1978 for its last season, and they continued their roles on both shows.
10) *I Spy* - starring Bill Cosby in 1965

Quiz 11

1) After *Doctor Who*, what is the second longest running science fiction or fantasy series?
2) What year did the BET network launch?
3) What year did FOX become the first new national television network since the 1950s?
4) What was the first streaming series to win the best drama Emmy?
5) What year was the first commercial color broadcast?
6) What did the acronym ESPN originally stand for?
7) Who was the first African American to win the Outstanding Supporting Actor in a Comedy Series Emmy?
8) What was advertised in the first U.S. television commercial?
9) What year were the first Emmy Awards?
10) Due to his early television success, who became known as Mr. Television and helped popularize the medium?

Quiz 11 Answers

1) *Supernatural* - debuted in 2005
2) 1980
3) 1993
4) *The Handmaid's Tale* – Hulu in 2017
5) 1951
6) Entertainment and Sports Programming Network
7) Robert Guillaume - *Soap* (1979)
8) Bulova watches
9) 1949

10) Milton Berle

Quiz 12

1) What show is generally credited with inventing the rerun?
2) What show has the most Emmy wins for a drama?
3) What comedy drama series featured a mansion that is the second largest private home ever built in the U.S.?
4) What show has the most Emmy wins for a comedy?
5) On *Doctor Who*, what planet is the Doctor from?
6) What series has the most Emmy wins in a single year?
7) Who was the first African American to ever win a primetime Emmy?
8) What is the longest running U.S. scripted primetime show of all time?
9) What year was the first paid television advertisement broadcast in the U.S.?
10) What was the first *Star Trek* series not filmed in the United States?

Quiz 12 Answers

1) *I Love Lucy* – during Lucille Ball's pregnancy
2) *Game of Thrones* (2011-2019)
3) *Royal Pains* (2009-2016) – The mansion that the character Boris Kuester von Jurgens-Ratenicz lived in is the 109,000 square foot Oheka Castle in West Hills, New York which was built from 1914-1919 for Otto Hermann Kahn. It is the second largest private home ever built in the U.S. after the Biltmore Estate in Asheville, North Carolina which is 175,856 square feet.
4) *Frasier* (1993-2004) – 37 wins
5) Gallifrey
6) *Game of Thrones* – 12 wins in both 2015 and 2016
7) Harry Belafonte – *Tonight with Harry Belafonte* (1960)
8) *The Simpsons* - started in 1989
9) 1941
10) *Star Trek: Discovery* – It debuted in 2017 and is filmed in Toronto, Canada.

Quiz 13

1) What is the only U.S. primetime series to be on for at least 14 years without winning an Emmy?

2) Which network holds the record for most primetime Emmy wins in a year?
3) What was the first television series to feature a final episode where all plot lines were resolved, and all questions were answered?
4) In what year was the first color television system demonstrated?
5) Who was the first African American to win the Outstanding Lead Actress in a Drama Series Emmy?
6) What year did *The Tonight Show* debut?
7) What television show cast holds the all-time record for most Billboard Hot 100 hit song entries?
8) Who was the first African American to win the Outstanding Supporting Actress in a Comedy Series Emmy?
9) What was the first soap opera to expand to 60 minutes?
10) What was the first R-rated series in the U.S.?

Quiz 13 Answers

1) *Supernatural* - debuted in 2005
2) CBS - 44 wins in 1974
3) *The Fugitive* - 1967
4) 1928
5) Viola Davis - *How to Get Away with Murder* (2015)
6) 1954
7) *Glee* - 207 entries
8) Jackee Harry - 227 (1987)
9) *Another World* - 1975
10) *NYPD Blue* – 1993

Quiz 14

1) What is Mickey Mouse's dog's name?
2) What star's baby appeared on the first cover of *TV Guide*?
3) What is the most widely watched PBS show ever worldwide?
4) What character's real name is Gordon Shumway?
5) In children's television, who is Lumpy Brannum better known as?
6) What is the only television show that was made into a Best Picture Oscar winner?
7) Bea Arthur costarred with what actress for 13 years over two different series?
8) What was the most watched U.S. series finale of all time?

9) What was the first primetime series starring a female private eye?
10) What year did Walt Disney have his first series?

Quiz 14 Answers

1) Pluto
2) Lucille Ball
3) *Cosmos* – with Carl Sagan
4) Alf
5) Mr. Green Jeans on *Captain Kangaroo*
6) *Marty* - 1955
7) Rue McClanahan - *Maude* and *The Golden Girls*
8) *M*A*S*H*
9) *Honey West* (1965-1966)
10) 1954 - *Disneyland* which later became *Walt Disney's Wonderful World of Color*

Quiz 15

1) How many series were spun off from *All in the Family*?
2) What was the first U.S. show to broadcast 1,000 episodes?
3) Who was the first African American woman to win a primetime acting Emmy?
4) Who was the first *Saturday Night Live* cast member to also have their child become a cast member?
5) Who was the first African American to win the Outstanding Lead Actress in a Comedy Series Emmy?
6) What American primetime scripted show has been the longest running show for the longest time?
7) What is the longest running live action primetime spinoff series ever on American television?
8) Who was the first African American to host a nationwide show?
9) How did the television awards get the name Emmys?
10) Who is the only Star Trek character to appear regularly on two different *Star Trek* series?

Quiz 15 Answers

1) Seven – *Maude, Good Times, The Jeffersons, Checking In, Archie Bunker's Place, Gloria, 704 Hauser*
2) *The Howdy Doody Show* (1947-1960)

3) Gail Fisher – *Mannix* (1970) for Outstanding Supporting Actress in a Drama Series

4) Chris Elliot

5) Isabel Sanford – *The Jeffersons* (1981)

6) *The Simpsons* – It has been the longest running show since July 1998.

7) *Law & Order: Special Victims Unit* – debuted in 1999

8) Nat King Cole – 1956

9) Immy was a term commonly used for the image orthicon tube used in early cameras; the name was feminized to Emmy to match the female statuette.

10) Worf – He was played by Michael Dorn and appeared on both *Star Trek: The Next Generation* and *Star Trek: Deep Space Nine.*

Quiz 16

1) What fictional character has been played by the most actors on film and television?

2) What is the longest running children's show in the U.S.?

3) What was the first 90-minute U.S. series?

4) What was the only U.S. fiction series shot all over the U.S. and Canada including episodes filmed in 40 different states?

5) Who was the first African American to win the Outstanding Lead Actor in a Drama Series Emmy?

6) What were the first Olympics broadcast anywhere?

7) Who created *Jeopardy!* and *Wheel of Fortune*?

8) What is the only action adventure show on U.S. television to have a historical setting and a female lead?

9) Who was the first regular character on U.S. television who was a divorcee?

10) Who was the youngest cast member ever on *Saturday Night Live*?

Quiz 16 Answers

1) Sherlock Holmes

2) *Sesame Street* – started in 1969

3) *The Virginian* – 1962

4) *Route 66* (1960–1964)

5) Bill Cosby – *I Spy* (1966)

6) Berlin – 1936

7) Merv Griffin

8) *Wonder Woman* (1975-1979) – starring Lynda Carter
9) Vivian Bagley - *The Lucy Show* (1962)
10) Anthony Michael Hall – 17 years old

Quiz 17

1) What 1950s sitcom is the only primetime series to run consecutively without interruption on three major televisions networks?
2) What show had the last theme song to make it to number one on Billboard's Hot 100?
3) Which three series have won Emmys for all their main cast members?
4) Who was the first African American to win the Outstanding Lead Actor in a Comedy Series Emmy?
5) What was the first U.S. network show without a theme song?
6) What was the first television family with a computer in their home?
7) What was the first nationally televised children's show in the U.S.?
8) What is the world's longest running talk show?
9) What show has the all-time Nielsen season average share rating record?
10) What was the first regularly scheduled network television service in the U.S.?

Quiz 17 Answers

1) *Bachelor Father* - CBS from 1957 to 1959, NBC from 1959 to 1961, ABC from 1961 to 1962
2) *Miami Vice* - "Theme from Miami Vice" in 1985
3) *All in the Family, The Golden Girls, Will & Grace*
4) Robert Guillaume - *Benson* (1985)
5) *60 Minutes*
6) *The Addams Family* - They had a huge UNIVAC computer.
7) *The Howdy Doody Show* (1947-1960)
8) *The Tonight Show* - started in 1954
9) *I Love Lucy* in 1953 - It had a Nielsen season average share of 67.3 meaning that on average 67.3% of all households viewing television were watching it.
10) NBC - 1945

Quiz 18

1) Who is generally credited with inventing the television as we know it and giving the world's first public demonstration of a true television set?
2) What year was the first *Today* broadcast?
3) What show has the highest number of performers nominated for lead, supporting, or guest actress or actor Emmys over its run?
4) Who was the first woman to anchor a U.S. network evening newscast?
5) What is the longest running variety show in the U.S.?
6) What long time *60 Minutes* correspondent hosted seven game shows early in his career?
7) What is the longest running animated show in the U.S.?
8) What was the first series set in Hawaii?
9) What was the first animated series after *The Flintstones* in 1961 to be nominated for the Outstanding Comedy Series Emmy?
10) What was the longest running *All in the Family* spinoff?

Quiz 18 Answers

1) John Logie Baird – He demonstrated a television set in 1926.
2) 1951
3) *ER* – 31 separate performers
4) Barbara Walters
5) *Saturday Night Live* – started in 1975
6) Mike Wallace
7) *The Simpsons* - started in 1989
8) *Hawaiian Eye* (1959-1963) – It wasn't filmed there.
9) *Family Guy* – 2009
10) *The Jeffersons* – 11 seasons from 1975-1985

Quiz 19

1) The Daleks from *Doctor Who* come from what planet?
2) What did President Ronald Reagan say was his favorite television show?
3) What is the longest running sitcom in the U.S.?
4) What was the first WWII series entirely filmed and broadcast in color?
5) What show had the first interracial couple on regular primetime

U.S. television?

6) Who is the youngest person to have a self-titled U.S. television show?

7) Who was the first U.S. president to be televised?

8) What three series are tied for the most consecutive Outstanding Drama Series Emmys at four?

9) What was the first Asian country to broadcast television?

10) According to a British Film Institute poll of industry professionals in 2000, what is the greatest British television series of all time?

Quiz 19 Answers

1) Skaro

2) *Family Ties*

3) *The Simpsons* - started in 1989

4) *Rat Patrol* (1966-1968)

5) *The Jeffersons* - neighbors Tom and Helen Willis in 1975

6) Patty Duke - She was 16 years old when *The Patty Duke Show* debuted in 1963.

7) Franklin D. Roosevelt - opening ceremonies of the 1939 New York World's Fair

8) *Hill Street Blues* (1981-1984), *The West Wing* (2000-2003), *Mad Men* (2008-2011)

9) Japan - 1939

10) *Fawlty Towers* – aired 12 episodes in the 1970s

1950s

Quiz 1

1) What comedy had a 20-year run with characters like Freddie the Freeloader?
2) What was Ralph's last name on *The Honeymooners*?
3) On *Bonanza*, before becoming a rancher, what was Ben Cartwright's occupation?
4) What show's main character has business cards showing a chess piece?
5) The Billboard Hot 100 number one song "Johnny Angel" debuted on what sitcom and was sung by the actress who played the daughter on the show?
6) What was the last name of the title character on the western *Cheyenne*?
7) Who played the neighbor Blanche Morton on *The George Burns and Gracie Allen Show*?
8) On *Richard Diamond, Private Detective*, a future famous actress played the role of Sam the switchboard operator who only ever had her legs and hands visible on camera; who played the role?
9) In *The Twilight Zone* episode "Time Enough at Last", who played the bookworm bank clerk who survives a nuclear holocaust?
10) What entertainer had two CBS weekly series and a daily 90-minute mid-morning show in the mid-1950s?

Quiz 1 Answers

1) *The Red Skelton Show* (1951-1971)
2) Kramden
3) Ship's captain
4) *Have Gun – Will Travel* (1957-1963)
5) *The Donna Reed Show* (1958-1966) – Shelley Fabares played the daughter and sang the song.
6) Bodie
7) Bea Benaderet – Kate Bradley on *Petticoat Junction*
8) Mary Tyler Moore
9) Burgess Meredith
10) Arthur Godfrey – *Arthur Godfrey's Talent Scouts, Arthur Godfrey and His*

Friends, Arthur Godfrey Time

Quiz 2

1) What is the name of the restaurant featured prominently in 77 *Sunset Strip* that was right next door to the private detective office?
2) Who took dictation from Perry Mason?
3) The actor who played Major Seth Adams, the leader on *Wagon Train*, died during the fourth season; who was he?
4) What was the first television western written for adults?
5) What is the first name of the grizzled old cook played by Frank McGrath on *Wagon Train*?
6) What two well-known children's shows both premiered on October 3, 1955 on different networks?
7) What series was based on James Stewart's radio series *The Six Shooter*?
8) In what series were the exterior shots of the family home the real home of the stars?
9) The Ponderosa ranch on *Bonanza* was located on the shores of what lake?
10) What anthology series was hosted by Ronald Reagan?

Quiz 2 Answers

1) Dino's Lodge – It was owned by Dean Martin at the time.
2) Della Street
3) Ward Bond
4) *The Life and Legend of Wyatt Earp* (1955-1961) – It premiered four days before *Gunsmoke* in 1955.
5) Charlie
6) *The Mickey Mouse Club* and *Captain Kangaroo*
7) *The Restless Gun* - It adapted some of the radio stories.
8) *The Adventures of Ozzie and Harriet* (1952-1966)
9) Lake Tahoe – The Ponderosa was supposedly 1,000 square miles (640,000 acres) on the eastern shore.
10) *General Electric Theater* (1953-1962)

Quiz 3

1) What show had the Muppets first television appearance?
2) What actors played the father and mother on *Father Knows Best*?

3) Who played the title role on *The Lone Ranger*?
4) What was the name of the family featured on *Father Knows Best*?
5) What were the first names of Beaver's mother and father on *Leave It to Beaver*?
6) Jack Benny's real-life wife frequently appeared with him on *The Jack Benny Program*; what was her name?
7) What kind of car did Jack Benny drive on *The Jack Benny Program*?
8) What famous bird first appeared on television in September 1957?
9) How many continuous years was *American Bandstand* on the air?
10) Who was the host and wrote the theme song for *The Mickey Mouse Club*?

Quiz 3 Answers

1) *The Ed Sullivan Show*
2) Robert Young and Jane Wyatt
3) Clayton Moore
4) Anderson
5) Ward and June
6) Mary Livingstone
7) Maxwell
8) NBC peacock
9) 37 years
10) Jimmie Dodd

Quiz 4

1) What popular western was one of the only television shows to spawn a radio show?
2) What show opened with "The story you are about to see is true. The names have been changed to protect the innocent"?
3) What sitcom featured the adventures of the scatterbrained wife of a city judge?
4) What was Beaver Cleaver's real first name?
5) Who was the host of *Candid Camera*?
6) What quiz show was the center of the 1950s scandal involving Charles Van Doren and Herb Stempel?
7) June Lockhart replaced what well known actress as the mother on *Lassie*?
8) What western had a huge following in Japan to the point that one

of its stars was invited to dinner with Japan's prime minister when he visited?

9) What award-winning songwriter appeared on the western *Laramie*?

10) Who was the host and star of *Texaco Star Theatre*?

Quiz 4 Answers

1) *Have Gun – Will Travel* (1957-1963) – The radio show started one year after the television show and reused stories.
2) *Dragnet* (1951-1959)
3) *I Married Joan* (1952-1955)
4) Theodore
5) Allen Funt
6) *Twenty-One* (1956-1958)
7) Cloris Leachman - She was on the show from 1957 to 1958.
8) *Laramie* (1959-1963)
9) Hoagy Carmichael - composer of "Stardust" and "Georgia on My Mind"
10) Milton Berle

Quiz 5

1) Who played the title role on *Bat Masterson*?
2) Who starred as Chief Dan Mathews on *Highway Patrol*?
3) On children's television, Hugh "Lumpy" Brannum played what well known character?
4) What long running children's show had Mr. Do-Bee, a friendly bumblebee who taught children polite behavior, and the Magic Mirror?
5) What act had the most appearances on *American Bandstand*?
6) What was the name of the *Daily Planet* editor on *Adventures of Superman*?
7) On *Bonanza*, who was the Ponderosa's Chinese cook?
8) Who sang the theme song for *Rawhide*?
9) Who was Dick Clark's sidekick and announcer on American Bandstand?
10) What was the name of Groucho Marx's game show?

Quiz 5 Answers

1) Gene Barry

2) Broderick Crawford
3) Mr. Green Jeans - *Captain Kangaroo*
4) *Romper Room* (1953-1994)
5) Freddy Cannon - 110 times
6) Perry White
7) Hop Sing
8) Frankie Laine
9) Charlie O'Donnell
10) *You Bet Your Life* (1950-1961)

Quiz 6

1) On *The Real McCoys*, who played grandfather Amos?
2) On what show did the character of Sheriff Andy Taylor first appear?
3) One of the creators of the game show *I've Got a Secret* was best known for his novelty songs; who was he?
4) Who was the only female comedy regular on *Your Show of Shows*?
5) What long running sitcom featured a real family?
6) What was the first American television series shown on British television?
7) What was Clint Eastwood's character name on *Rawhide*?
8) The characters on *The Honeymooners* first appeared on what show?
9) What actor and actress played the mother and father on *Leave It to Beaver*?
10) What were the names of the two sons on *The Adventures of Ozzie and Harriet*?

Quiz 6 Answers

1) Walter Brennan
2) *Make Room for Daddy* (1953-1965) - starring Danny Thomas
3) Allan Sherman - writer and singer of "Hello Muddah, Hello Fadduh" and other songs
4) Imogene Coca
5) *The Adventures of Ozzie and Harriet* (1952-1966)
6) *Dragnet*
7) Rowdy Yates
8) *The Jackie Gleason Show* (1952-1959) - It featured sketches with *The Honeymooners*.
9) Hugh Beaumont and Barbara Billingsley

10) Ricky and David

Quiz 7

1) Who played the title role on the western *Cheyenne*?
2) What panelist appeared the most times on the game show *What's My Line*?
3) Who played the title character on *Have Gun - Will Travel*?
4) Who played Alice on *The Honeymooners*?
5) Who was the first host of *Truth or Consequences* on television?
6) On *Bachelor Father*, a bachelor raises his teenage niece with the help of his manservant; who played the title role?
7) Who played the title role on *The Life of Riley*?
8) What quiz show made a celebrity out of psychologist Joyce Brothers as a winning contestant answering questions about boxing?
9) Carl Betz played the father on *The Donna Reed Show*; what was his occupation?
10) On *Captain Kangaroo*, who created and appeared as Mr. Moose and Bunny Rabbit and played Dennis the Apprentice, Dancing Bear, Grandfather Clock, and was the artist behind the Magic Drawing Board?

Quiz 7 Answers

1) Clint Walker
2) Arlene Francis
3) Richard Boone
4) Audrey Meadows
5) Ralph Edwards
6) John Forsythe
7) William Bendix
8) *The $64,000 Question* (1955-1958)
9) Doctor – pediatrician
10) Cosmo Allegretti

Quiz 8

1) What western featured gambling brothers Bret and Bart?
2) Who was the narrator for *The Untouchables*?
3) What CBS anthology series attracted many top directors and actors?
4) Twenty-two-year-old Warren Beatty got his start playing Milton

Armitage on what sitcom?

5) Who played Tonto on *The Lone Ranger*?

6) Who played Eliot Ness on *The Untouchables*?

7) What series had lines such as "I hope you'll join us again next week, when we will present you with another story of gripping, spine-tingling suspense, and three boring commercials to take the edge off of it"?

8) What 1951-1972 children's show featured science experiments?

9) On *December Bride*, who played neighbor Pete Porter who complained constantly about his unseen wife Gladys?

10) What was the original title of *The Ed Sullivan Show* from 1948 until 1955?

Quiz 8 Answers

1) *Maverick* (1957-1962) – starring James Garner and Jack Kelly

2) Walter Winchell

3) *Playhouse 90* (1956-1961)

4) *The Many Loves of Dobie Gillis* (1959-1963)

5) Jay Silverheels

6) Robert Stack

7) *Alfred Hitchcock Presents* (1955-1962)

8) *Watch Mr. Wizard*

9) Harry Morgan

10) *Toast of the Town*

Quiz 9

1) Ben Alexander played Jack Webb's partner on *Dragnet* for most of the 1950s; what was his character name?

2) What children's show featured a Claymation duo?

3) Where did the name Paladin come from in *Have Gun - Will Travel*?

4) Danny Thomas played a nightclub singer balancing career and family on what show?

5) What series ended in 1959 with the unexpected death of its lead actor?

6) *This Is Your Life* surprised a celebrity each week and told the story of their life; who was the host?

7) What was the Lone Ranger's real name?

8) Who played Davy Crockett in a five-part *Disneyland* miniseries?

9) What was the name of the town where the Cleavers lived on *Leave It to Beaver*?

10) On *Bonanza*, Hoss is a nickname; what is the character's real first name?

Quiz 9 Answers

1) Frank Smith
2) *The Gumby Show* (1957-1968) – with his horse Pokey
3) The Paladins were the 12 knights in Charlemagne's court in the 8th century; over time, paladin has come to mean generically a knight, warrior, or chivalrous person.
4) *Make Room for Daddy* (1953-1965)
5) *Adventures of Superman* - George Reeves died of a gunshot wound to the head.
6) Ralph Edwards
7) John Reid
8) Fess Parker
9) Mayfield
10) Eric

Quiz 10

1) What children's show had the cartoon *Tom Terrific with Mighty Manfred the Wonder Dog*?
2) What was the name of the cook on *Rawhide*?
3) Who played the title role on *Richard Diamond, Private Detective*?
4) What were the names of Lucy and Ricky's landlords and friends on *I Love Lucy*?
5) Who played *Captain Kangaroo*?
6) To boost ratings in 1953, the *Today* show hired a chimpanzee that played the piano and did acrobatics; what was his name?
7) What character did Chuck Connors play on *The Rifleman*?
8) Gale Gordon played the principal on *Our Miss Brooks*; what was his character name?
9) What was the name of the saloon on *Gunsmoke*?
10) Eric Fleming played the trail boss on Rawhide; what was his character name?

Quiz 10 Answers

1) *Captain Kangaroo* (1955-1992)
2) Wishbone
3) David Janssen
4) Fred and Ethel Mertz
5) Bob Keeshan
6) J. Fred Muggs
7) Lucas McCain
8) Osgood Conklin
9) Long Branch
10) Gil Favor

Quiz 11

1) Pete Nolan, one of the regular characters on *Rawhide*, was played by an actor who was also a singer and had a number one hit song; who was he?
2) Who played the title role on *Adventures of Superman*?
3) What detective show set in Hawaii featured Robert Conrad and Connie Stevens?
4) Who played the English cousin Beau on *Maverick*?
5) Where did Kangaroo come from in Captain Kangaroo's name?
6) Who played the lead character Vint Bonner on *The Restless Gun*?
7) What was the first name of the son of the title character on *The Rifleman*?
8) What was the name of the family on *Lassie*?
9) Who played Maynard G. Krebs on *The Many Loves of Dobie Gillis*?
10) What character did Hank Ketcham create?

Quiz 11 Answers

1) Sheb Wooley - "The Purple People Eater" in 1958
2) George Reeves
3) *Hawaiian Eye* (1959-1963)
4) Roger Moore
5) He had large pouch like pockets in his coat.
6) John Payne
7) Mark
8) Martin

9) Bob Denver
10) Dennis the Menace

Quiz 12

1) In *Have Gun - Will Travel*, what city did Paladin live in?
2) What show had a soundtrack album that was number one on the Billboard chart and won two Grammys?
3) The Canadian comedy team of Johnny Wayne and Frank Shuster were on *The Ed Sullivan Show* the most times with 58 appearances; what act had the second most appearances?
4) Who played Corporal Rocco Barbella on *The Phil Silvers Show* and went on to play Eric Von Zipper in a series of 1960s beach movies?
5) On *Private Secretary*, who played the title role of Susie McNamara, secretary to talent agent Peter Sands?
6) What was the last name of the family on *The Donna Reed Show*?
7) What writer, producer, director, and actor who went on to create a very successful movie franchise was the creator of the private detective show *Peter Gunn*?
8) What future movie star played the role of blacksmith Quint Asper on *Gunsmoke*?
9) Who played the original Clarabell the Clown on *The Howdy Doody Show*?
10) On the original *Dragnet*, Joe Friday never said "Just the facts, ma'am"; what did he say instead?

Quiz 12 Answers

1) San Francisco
2) *Peter Gunn* (1958-1961) - music by Henry Mancini
3) Topo Gigio - Italian mouse puppet
4) Harvey Lembeck
5) Ann Sothern
6) Stone
7) Blake Edwards - *Pink Panther* creator and director
8) Burt Reynolds
9) Bob Keeshan - He went on to play Captain Kangaroo.
10) All we want to know are the facts, ma'am

Quiz 13

1) What show had a famous director introducing short stories that covered a variety of genres?
2) What was the name of the ranch on *The Roy Rogers Show*?
3) What was the name of the sister quartet that appeared on *The Lawrence Welk Show*?
4) What show featured Marilyn Monroe's first television appearance?
5) What was the name of Hopalong Cassidy's horse?
6) What western featured correspondence school law graduate Tom Brewster traveling west to seek his fortune?
7) On *The Roy Rogers Show*, what was the name of Dale Evans' horse?
8) Who was the moderator for the game show *I've Got a Secret*?
9) On *77 Sunset Strip*, what was the character name of the restaurant valet played by Edd Byrnes?
10) On most *Perry Mason* episodes, the climactic courtroom scene wasn't part of the trial but was a preliminary hearing to decide whether to bind the defendant over for trial; what was the practical reason for this?

Quiz 13 Answers

1) *Alfred Hitchcock Presents* (1955–1962)
2) Double R Ranch
3) The Lennon Sisters
4) *The Jack Benny Program* – 1953
5) Topper
6) *Sugarfoot* (1957–1961)
7) Buttermilk
8) Garry Moore
9) Kookie
10) They didn't have to hire 12 extras to play a jury.

Quiz 14

1) Even though he was in his late 20s when the series started, who played the squeaky voiced high school student Walter Denton on *Our Miss Brooks*?
2) On *Leave It to Beaver*, what was Wally's best friend's name?
3) The catchphrase "What a revoltin' development this is!" was from what show?

4) What long running show frequently used the word "wunnerful"?
5) Who played agent Jim Hardie on *Tales of Wells Fargo*?
6) Until it was passed by *The Simpsons* in 2004, what was the longest running American sitcom in history?
7) What was Chester Riley's job on *The Life of Riley*?
8) Who played Doc Adams on *Gunsmoke*?
9) Who played the title role on *Dennis the Menace*?
10) Who played grandson Luke McCoy on *The Real McCoys*?

Quiz 14 Answers

1) Richard Crenna
2) Eddie Haskell
3) *The Life of Riley* (1953–1958) – spoken by Chester Riley
4) *The Lawrence Welk Show* (1955–1982)
5) Dale Robertson
6) *The Adventures of Ozzie and Harriet* – 14 seasons
7) Riveter in an aircraft plant
8) Milburn Stone
9) Jay North
10) Richard Crenna

Quiz 15

1) Who was the real-life owner and trainer of *Lassie*?
2) Who was the announcer on *The Jack Benny Program*?
3) On *I Love Lucy*, what was the name of the club where Ricky worked?
4) On *The Texan*, a Civil War veteran with a reputation of being the fastest gun in the west roams across Texas; who played the title role?
5) Who played the title role on *The Life and Legend of Wyatt Earp*?
6) What show featured Arthur Godfrey searching for talent with a winner declared by the audience?
7) On *The Phil Silvers Show*, what was Sergeant Bilko's job in the army?
8) What show started with "A fiery horse with the speed of light, a cloud of dust"?
9) What was the name of the district attorney on *Perry Mason*?
10) On *Dennis the Menace*, what was Dennis' last name?

Quiz 15 Answers

1) Rudd Weatherwax
2) Don Wilson
3) Tropicana
4) Rory Calhoun
5) Hugh O'Brian
6) *Arthur Godfrey's Talent Scouts*
7) He ran the motor pool.
8) *The Lone Ranger*
9) Hamilton Burger – a word play on hamburger
10) Mitchell

Quiz 16

1) Ken Curtis played the deputy on *Gunsmoke* longer than anyone else; what was his full character name?
2) What was Zorro's real name?
3) What line follows "You are traveling through another dimension, a dimension not only of sight and sound but of mind. A journey into a wondrous land of imagination"?
4) What was the name of the Cisco Kid's sidekick?
5) What is the name of Tonto's horse on *The Lone Ranger*?
6) Who played the title role on *The Cisco Kid*?
7) Who had his own comedy variety show and was known as "Lonesome George"?
8) What series starred Lloyd Bridges as scuba diver Mike Nelson?
9) What show popularized and may have originated the phrase "Whoa Nelly!"?
10) Who played the title character on *Hopalong Cassidy*?

Quiz 16 Answers

1) Festus Haggen
2) Don Diego de la Vega
3) Next stop, the Twilight Zone!
4) Pancho
5) Scout
6) Duncan Renaldo
7) George Gobel – *The George Gobel Show* was on from 1954-1960.

8) *Sea Hunt* (1958–1961)

9) *The Roy Rogers Show* (1951–1957) – On nearly every show, Pat Brady would yell the phrase while racing after villains or rushing for help in his Jeep named Nellybelle.

10) William Boyd

Quiz 17

1) What town was *Father Knows Best* set in?

2) On the television version of *Marty* on the *Goodyear TV Playhouse* that inspired the movie, who played the title role?

3) On the entire *Bonanza* series, how many total times did the Cartwright's propose marriage?

4) Who played the lead character, a bounty hunter, on *Wanted: Dead or Alive*?

5) On *The Millionaire*, what was the name of the millionaire who gives people he doesn't know a million dollars?

6) Who was the host on *The Howdy Doody Show*?

7) What was Ralph's occupation on *The Honeymooners*?

8) What comedy sketch show featured the writing of Neil Simon and Mel Brooks?

9) What was the name of Dennis the Menace's dog?

10) What was the name of the Cisco Kid's horse?

Quiz 17 Answers

1) Springfield

2) Rod Steiger

3) 22 times – Little Joe (11), Hoss (6), Ben (3), Adam (2)

4) Steve McQueen

5) John Beresford Tipton

6) Buffalo Bob Smith

7) Bus driver

8) *Your Show of Shows* (1950–1954)

9) Ruff

10) Diablo

Quiz 18

1) Who played the title role on *Our Miss Brooks*?

2) On *The Honeymooners*, what was Ed Norton's occupation?

3) On *The Twilight Zone* episode "It's a Good Life", who played the six-year-old boy who can read thoughts and wish people off to the cornfield?

4) Who used to say, "Hey, Eddie, kees me goodnight"?

5) What was Lucy's maiden name on *I Love Lucy*?

6) Who wrote the novels on which *Perry Mason* was based?

7) What sitcom featured the misadventures of an English teacher at Madison High?

8) Who was the accordionist who appeared on every episode of *The Lawrence Welk Show*?

9) Who was the announcer on the game show *You Bet Your Life*?

10) Jackie Gleason's character on *The Honeymooners* inspired what cartoon character in 1960?

Quiz 18 Answers

1) Eva Arden
2) Sewer worker
3) Billy Mumy
4) Topo Gigio – Italian mouse puppet who appeared on *The Ed Sullivan Show*
5) McGillicuddy
6) Erle Stanley Gardner
7) *Our Miss Brooks*
8) Myron Floren
9) George Fenneman
10) Fred Flintstone

Quiz 19

1) What sitcom at various times starred Ethel Waters, Louise Beavers, and Hattie McDaniel in the title role as a servant who pulls the family together?

2) What science fiction adventure had Commander Corey and youthful Cadet Happy roaming the 30th century universe in their ship *Terra* fighting villains?

3) What science fiction adventure was set in the middle of the 24th century at the Space Academy training school for the Solar Guards and was one of the very few programs to air on all four major networks?

4) What was Gene Autry's horse's name on *The Gene Autry Show*?

5) There were four major television networks in the 1950s; they were ABC, NBC, CBS, and what?

6) On *The Paul Winchell Show*, ventriloquist Paul Winchell starred with his dummy; what was his dummy's name?

7) What game show had couples competing to win prizes by completing stunts within a time limit?

8) What show responded to viewer requests to see things like looking into the Fort Knox vaults?

9) What comedy hour featured many notable comedians and entertainers of the era and was Woody Allen's television debut?

10) What series featured primarily adaptations of motion pictures with Hollywood stars and a host who would introduce each production and interview the stars after?

Quiz 19 Answers

1) *Beulah* (1950–1953)
2) *Space Patrol* (1950–1955)
3) *Tom Corbett, Space Cadet* (1950–1955)
4) Champion
5) DuMont Television Network
6) Jerry Mahoney
7) *Beat the Clock* (1950–1961)
8) *You Asked for It* (1950–1959)
9) *The Colgate Family Hour* (1950–1955)
10) *Lux Video Theatre* (1950–1959)

1960s

Quiz 1

1) What was the occupation of Marlo Thomas' boyfriend on *That Girl*?
2) On *F-Troop*, what was the name of the fort?
3) Who played police officer Francis Muldoon on *Car 54, Where Are You*?
4) What was the name of Barbara Stanwyck's character on *The Big Valley*?
5) Who played the banker Mr. Mooney on *The Lucy Show*?
6) What cartoon character and gang leader lived in Hoagy's Alley?
7) What fashion craze was Mary Tyler Moore responsible for based on her role on *The Dick Van Dyke Show*?
8) What were the names of the two spy agencies on *Get Smart*?
9) Poopdeck Pappy was what character's father?
10) What series starred Vince Edwards as a doctor fighting against the medical establishment?

Quiz 1 Answers

1) Magazine reporter
2) Fort Courage
3) Fred Gwynne
4) Victoria Barkley
5) Gale Gordon
6) Top Cat
7) Capri pants - She wore them almost exclusively on the show.
8) CONTROL and KAOS - They were supposed to be acronyms, but Mel Brooks and Buck Henry who were the writers on the show never came up with anything for them to stand for.
9) Popeye
10) *Ben Casey* (1961–1966)

Quiz 2

1) Who played the title role on *My Favorite Martian*?
2) The office on *The Dick Van Dyke Show* is based on Carl Reiner's experience on *Your Show of Shows* where he worked as a writer; Dick Van Dyke's character was based on Carl Reiner; Morey Amsterdam's character of Buddy Sorrell was based on what famous

writer, director and actor who was also a writer on *Your Show of Shows*?

3) What were the names of the two main characters on *The Wild West*?

4) What series starred Patrick McGoohan as John Drake, a special operative for NATO?

5) On *Get Smart*, what was Maxwell Smart's agent number?

6) Fred Flintstone's "Yabba-dabba-doo" was inspired by what well known advertising slogan?

7) On *Star Trek*, what was Captain Kirk's middle name?

8) To capitalize on the popularity of creepy comedies like *The Addams Family* and *The Munsters*, what show introduced Weirdly and Creepella Gruesome as neighbors?

9) On *Gilligan's Island*, the character name Thurston Howell III was based on a similar character also played by Jim Backus on what show?

10) What series had three rotating stars played by Gene Barry, Robert Stack, and Anthony Franciosa who were featured on independent episodes tied together by a connection to a publishing company?

Quiz 2 Answers

1) Ray Walston
2) Mel Brooks
3) James West and Artemus Gordon
4) *Danger Man* (1960-1962)
5) 86
6) Brylcreem's "A little dab'll do you" – The mother of the actor who voiced Fred liked to say the Brylcreem slogan, so he suggested it to the creators.
7) Tiberius
8) *The Flintstones* (1960-1966)
9) *The Alan Young Show* – Backus played Hubert Updike III on the show which was also written by Sherwood Schwartz, creator of *Gilligan's Island*.
10) *The Name of the Game* (1968-1971)

Quiz 3

1) Who played the title role on *The Fugitive*?
2) On *The Munsters*, what is the name of Eddie's pet dragon that lives under the stairs?

3) What was the name of the ranger who is always after Yogi Bear?

4) On *McHale's Navy*, who played the bumbling Ensign Parker?

5) What was the nearest town to the Barkley Ranch on *The Big Valley*?

6) What show starred Ben Gazzara as a lawyer who is told he only has two years to live?

7) Who was the only actor or actress to play two different criminal roles on *Batman*?

8) Who was Underdog in love with?

9) What western featured the Cannon family in the 1870s Arizona territory?

10) Charles Addams' *New Yorker* cartoons of a spooky husband and wife were the inspiration for *The Addams Family* and what famous cartoon villain duo?

Quiz 3 Answers

1) David Janssen
2) Spot
3) Ranger Smith
4) Tim Conway
5) Stockton, California
6) *Run for Your Life* (1965–1968)
7) Anne Baxter - Olga and Zelda
8) Sweet Polly Purebred
9) *The High Chaparral* (1967–1971)
10) Boris Badenov and Natasha Fatale – *Rocky and Bullwinkle*

Quiz 4

1) Which U.S. president did the agents work for on *The Wild Wild West*?

2) What show followed the work of Pete Malloy and Jim Reed?

3) Where was Bullwinkle Moose originally from?

4) What series featured Mia Farrow, Ryan O'Neal, Dorothy Malone, and Ed Nelson?

5) *The Green Hornet* was the alter ego for what character?

6) What Hollywood legend played Robert Wagner's father in a recurring role on *It Takes a Thief*?

7) Who played Sally Rogers on *The Dick Van Dyke Show*?

8) On *The Flintstones*, Dino was Fred's pet; what was Barney's pet called?

9) What was the full character name of the vampire on the cult soap opera *Dark Shadows*?

10) Charles Boyer inspired what cartoon character?

Quiz 4 Answers

1) Ulysses S. Grant
2) *Adam-12* (1968–1975)
3) Moosylvania – It is a small island in Lake of the Woods that neither the U.S. nor Canada wants to claim.
4) *Peyton Place* (1964–1969)
5) Britt Reid
6) Fred Astaire
7) Rose Marie
8) Hoppy – a hoparoo
9) Barnabas Collins
10) Pepe le Pew – the skunk

Quiz 5

1) What were the character names of the six children on *The Brady Bunch*?
2) On *The Patty Duke Show*, what was the reason given that Patty and her cousin looked so much alike?
3) What show opened with "There is nothing wrong with your television set. Do not attempt to adjust the picture"?
4) While the Grinch was stealing Christmas on *How the Grinch Stole Christmas!*, what was the name of the little girl he wakes up?
5) On *The Beverly Hillbillies*, who was Mr. Drysdale's secretary?
6) What was the name of the son on *The Jetsons*?
7) What series was based on a best-selling book and movie of the same name and featured the Nash family with a college English professor father, a newspaper columnist mother, and their four rambunctious sons, and a huge sheep dog?
8) On *The Munsters*, what was Lily's maiden name?
9) What was the name of Samantha's cousin who was also played by Elizabeth Montgomery on *Bewitched*?
10) What well known disc jockey, radio personality, voice actor and actor provided the voice for Shaggy on *Scooby Doo, Where Are You*?

Quiz 5 Answers

1) Marcia, Jan, Cindy, Greg, Peter, Bobby
2) Their fathers were identical twins.
3) *The Outer Limits* (1963-1965)
4) Cindy Lou Who
5) Jane Hathaway
6) Elroy
7) *Please Don't Eat the Daisies* (1965-1967)
8) Dracula
9) Serena
10) Casey Kasem

Quiz 6

1) Who were the two actors who played Darrin Stephens on *Bewitched*?
2) The actor who voiced the title character on the animated series *Jonny Quest* was 17 at the time and went on to a long acting career; who is he?
3) What was the name of the Green Hornet's car?
4) Where does Yogi bear live?
5) Who provided the voices of Bugs Bunny, Sylvester, and Tweety Pie?
6) The cartoon character Mr. Peabody was modeled after what actor?
7) On *Bewitched*, what was the name of the character played by Agnes Moorehead?
8) What *Batman* villain had the real name Oswald Chesterfield Cobblepot?
9) The actress who provided the voice for the mother, Jane Jetson, on *The Jetsons* was best known for her starring role as what famous character in a series of 28 movies from 1938-1950?
10) Who played the title role on the private detective series *Honey West*?

Quiz 6 Answers

1) Dick York and Dick Sargent
2) Tim Matheson
3) Black Beauty
4) Jellystone Park
5) Mel Blanc
6) Clifton Webb

7) Endora
8) Penguin
9) Blondie Bumstead – Penny Singleton played Blondie and provided the voice for Jane Jetson.
10) Anne Francis

Quiz 7

1) What was the last name of the central family on *Flipper*?
2) What cartoon character was the fastest mouse in all of Mexico?
3) What was the occupation of Uncle Bill on *Family Affair*?
4) What show features Robert Wagner as cat burglar Alexander Mundy?
5) Where was *The Flying Nun* set?
6) Ted Cassidy, who played Lurch on *The Addams Family*, also played what other role on the show?
7) What was the name of the nosy female neighbor on *Bewitched*?
8) On *Mister Ed*, what was Ed's owner's full name?
9) Who played Mrs. Muir on *The Ghost & Mrs. Muir*?
10) Which of the *Mission Impossible* actors appeared in the most episodes?

Quiz 7 Answers

1) Ricks
2) Speedy Gonzalez
3) Engineer
4) *It Takes a Thief* (1968–1970)
5) Puerto Rico
6) Thing – the hand
7) Gladys Kravitz
8) Wilbur Post
9) Hope Lange
10) Greg Morris appeared in 171 episodes, the most of any actor. Peter Graves did not appear in season one.

Quiz 8

1) What cartoon character was born in a warren under the Brooklyn Dodgers' stadium?
2) What was the name of the series that was a continuation of *The*

Andy Griffith Show?

3) The maiden names of what two cartoon characters were Slaghoople and McBricker?

4) On *The Munsters*, what was the name of the normal niece?

5) What was the full name of Eddie Albert's character on *Green Acres*?

6) What was the first name of Oliver and Lisa's hired hand on *Green Acres*?

7) Who played Agent 99 on *Get Smart*?

8) What was the name of the long-time assistance and sidekick who eventually took over as host of *Mutual of Omaha's Wild Kingdom*?

9) Who played the title role on *Hazel*?

10) What was the name of the Irwin Allen series about a sub-orbital spaceship on a flight from Los Angeles to London that becomes lost when it passes through a strange cloud and lands on an alternate Earth like planet?

Quiz 8 Answers

1) Bugs Bunny
2) *Mayberry R.F.D.* (1968–1971)
3) Wilma Flintstone and Betty Rubble
4) Marilyn
5) Oliver Wendell Douglas
6) Eb
7) Barbara Feldon
8) Jim Fowler
9) Shirley Booth
10) *Land of the Giants* (1968–1970)

Quiz 9

1) Who was the only cast member to win an award for *Green Acres*?

2) What were the first names of the three members of *The Mod Squad*?

3) The Great Gazoo was an alien on what cartoon series?

4) What town was Gomer Pyle from on *Gomer Pyle: USMC*?

5) On *The Lucy Show*, what was Lucy's last name?

6) Which *Hawaii Five-O* actor was a real-life Honolulu police officer prior to acting?

7) On *The Jetsons*, George Jetson worked at Spacely Sprockets; what was the company name of their competitor?

8) What was the name of Lucille Ball's character on *Here's Lucy*, her third network sitcom which started in 1968?

9) In what western did Chuck Connors play Jason McCord who was court-martialed and kicked out of the army because of his alleged cowardice and traveled the west trying to restore his good name and reputation?

10) What was the name of Buffy's doll on *Family Affair*?

Quiz 9 Answers

1) Arnold the pig – He won a Patsy Award for best animal performance in 1967.

2) Pete, Linc, Julie

3) *The Flintstones*

4) Mayberry, North Carolina – The show was a spinoff from *The Andy Griffith Show*.

5) Carmichael

6) Kam Fong who played Det. Chin Ho Kelley was a Honolulu police officer from 1946-1962.

7) Cogswell Cogs

8) Lucy Carter

9) *Branded* (1965-1966)

10) Mrs. Beasley

Quiz 10

1) Gene Barry played a Los Angeles chief of detectives who was also a millionaire and lived a high-wheeling lifestyle on what series?

2) Pat Buttram played what character on *Green Acres*?

3) Who became a genius whenever he put on the fabulous Kerwood Derby?

4) Bamboo Harvester was the real name of the actor who played what character?

5) Who was Dudley Do-Right's nemesis?

6) Clint Howard appeared with his brother Ron on several episodes of *The Andy Griffith Show* and later starred on what series?

7) What was the character name of the teacher who played Andy's romantic interest on *The Andy Griffith Show*?

8) Wile E. Coyote got all his traps to try to catch the Roadrunner from what company?

9) What was the name of the suburb where Rob and Laura lived on *The

Dick Van Dyke Show?
10) What author created the character of *The Saint?*

Quiz 10 Answers

1) *Burke's Law* (1963-1966)
2) Mr. Haney
3) Bullwinkle Moose
4) Mister Ed
5) Snidely Whiplash
6) *Gentle Ben* (1967-1969)
7) Helen Crump
8) Acme
9) New Rochelle, New York
10) Leslie Charteris – He wrote a long series of books and stories featuring The Saint starting in the 1930s.

Quiz 11

1) What was the name of the house where Mrs. Muir lived with her children on *The Ghost & Mrs. Muir?*
2) David Soul and Bobby Sherman played logging brothers on *Here Come the Brides*; where was the show set?
3) How long was the original mission of *Star Trek's Enterprise* supposed to be?
4) What series was set in the Los Angeles area and featured Dr. Paul Lochner and Dr. Joe Gannon in a hospital complex?
5) *Mission Impossible* star Peter Graves was the real-life brother of what famous television actor?
6) What show featured Clarence, the Cross-Eyed Lion?
7) What was the name of Fred Flintstone's paper boy?
8) Who played the title role on *Marcus Welby, M.D.?*
9) Who played the title role on *Mannix?*
10) Who played the title role on the cult classic *The Prisoner?*

Quiz 11 Answers

1) Gull Cottage
2) Seattle – It was based on *Seven Brides for Seven Brothers.*
3) Five years
4) *Medical Center* (1969-1976)

5) James Arness – Matt Dillon of *Gunsmoke*
6) *Daktari* (1966–1969)
7) Arnold
8) Robert Young
9) Mike Connors
10) Patrick McGoohan

Quiz 12

1) Which *Hogan's Heroes* actor was a real survivor of the Holocaust?
2) In the original pilot for *Gilligan's Island*, who composed the theme song?
3) What was the name of the housekeeper played by Miyoshi Umeki on *The Courtship of Eddie's Father*?
4) What prop was used as Dr. McCoy's medical scanner on *Star Trek*?
5) Who played Kato on *The Green Hornet*?
6) What western took place on the Shiloh ranch in Medicine Bow, Wyoming?
7) On *Petticoat Junction*, which daughter was the real-life daughter of the show's creator?
8) What were the character first names of the original *My Three Sons*?
9) Who played the title role on *Julia* about a widowed nurse?
10) What was Batman's butler Alfred's last name?

Quiz 12 Answers

1) Robert Clary – played LeBeau
2) John Williams – The original song was replaced.
3) Mrs. Livingston
4) Salt shaker
5) Bruce Lee
6) *The Virginian* (1962–1971)
7) Betty Jo – She was played by Linda Henning, daughter of the show's creator Paul Henning.
8) Mike, Robbie, Chip – Ernie joined later after Mike left due to marriage; sister Dodie was added after Steven remarried.
9) Diahann Carroll
10) Pennyworth

Quiz 13

1) Who was the only American in the group on *Monty Python's Flying Circus*?
2) On *Petticoat Junction*, what was the name of the hotel?
3) On *Mission Impossible*, the team worked for the IMF; what did IMF stand for?
4) Who played Dr. McCoy on the original *Star Trek* series?
5) In *How the Grinch Stole Christmas!*, what was the name of the Grinch's dog?
6) What century was the setting for *Star Trek*?
7) In *The Man from U.N.C.L.E.*, what does U.N.C.L.E. stand for?
8) Who were the actresses who played John Steed's partner on *The Avengers* before and after Diana Rigg?
9) Roy Thinnes played David Vincent in what science fiction series?
10) What was Rob and Laura's last name on *The Dick Van Dyke Show*?

Quiz 13 Answers

1) Terry Gilliam – He was born in Minnesota.
2) Shady Rest
3) Impossible Missions Force
4) DeForest Kelley
5) Max
6) 23rd century
7) United Network Command for Law and Enforcement
8) Honor Blackman (before) and Linda Thorson (after)
9) *The Invaders* (1967–1968)
10) Petrie

Quiz 14

1) At the time they were cast, which of *The Monkees* were musicians?
2) What was the name of the friend that Lucy lived with on *The Lucy Show*?
3) What was the Professor's real character name on *Gilligan's Island*?
4) Who provided the narration on *The Fugitive*?
5) What was the name of the WWII drama series following an American infantry squad starring Vic Morrow?
6) What was cartoon character Mr. Peabody's first name?

7) What was the first name of the housekeeper on *The Brady Bunch*?

8) The actor who sang "You're a Mean One, Mr. Grinch" in *How the Grinch Stole Christmas!*, is best known as the voice of what character in many commercials?

9) Where was the WWII series *Rat Patrol* set?

10) Who played the title role on *The Virginian*?

Quiz 14 Answers

1) Peter Tork and Michael Nesmith
2) Vivian Bagley
3) Roy Hinkley
4) William Conrad
5) *Combat!* (1962–1967)
6) Hector
7) Alice
8) Tony the Tiger – Frosted Flakes
9) North Africa
10) James Drury

Quiz 15

1) On *Gilligan's Island*, the *S.S. Minnow* was named after who or what?

2) What was the name of Richard Deacon's character who was Alan Brady's brother-in-law on *The Dick Van Dyke Show*?

3) What was the name of the family dog on *My Three Sons*?

4) What mountain range did the Clampetts of *The Beverly Hillbillies* come from?

5) What sitcom was based on the novel *The Fifteenth Pelican*?

6) Who played Goober Pyle on *The Andy Griffith Show*?

7) According to the theme song for *The Patty Duke Show*, where did Patty live?

8) On *Hawaii Five-O*, what does the Five-O refer to?

9) On *Green Acres*, what was Arnold the pig's last name?

10) What was the first name of Carol Burnett's character on "The Family" sketches on *The Carol Burnett Show*?

Quiz 15 Answers

1) Newton Minow, head of the Federal Communications Commission (FCC) - Sherwood Schwartz, the show's creator did not care for

Minow who had called television "America's vast wasteland", so he named the soon to be shipwrecked ship after him.

2) Mel Cooley
3) Tramp
4) Ozarks
5) *The Flying Nun* (1967-1970)
6) George Lindsey
7) Brooklyn Heights
8) Hawaii being the 50th state
9) Ziffel
10) Eunice

Quiz 16

1) How many seconds elapsed before the tape self-destructed on *Mission Impossible*?
2) What was the name of the butler played by Sebastian Cabot on *Family Affair*?
3) Who lived at 0001 Cemetery Lane?
4) Who played Sgt. Morgan O'Rourke on *F Troop*?
5) Who was the host of *The Hollywood Squares*?
6) What was the name of George of the Jungle's pet elephant?
7) Where was the series *Gentle Ben* set?
8) What was the name of the police detective who chased Dr. Richard Kimble on *The Fugitive*?
9) Who played Dr. Welby's young assistant, Dr. Steven Kiley, on *Marcus Welby, M.D.*?
10) What future primetime soap star played young Audra Barkley on *The Big Valley*?

Quiz 16 Answers

1) Five seconds
2) Mr. French
3) *Addams Family*
4) Forrest Tucker
5) Peter Marshall
6) Shep
7) Florida Everglades
8) Lt. Philip Gerard

9) James Brolin

10) Linda Evans – She later starred in *Dynasty*.

Quiz 17

1) What was the character name of the head of U.N.C.L.E. on *The Man from U.N.C.L.E.*?

2) What was the name of the POW camp on *Hogan Heroes*?

3) What was Marlo Thomas' character's name on *That Girl*?

4) In what year was *Lost in Space* set?

5) What were the first names of the two brothers on the controversial *The Smothers Brothers Comedy Hour*?

6) On *Rocky and Bullwinkle*, what was Boris and Natasha's homeland?

7) Prior to the war, what was the job of Sergeant Schultz of *Hogan's Heroes*?

8) What were the first names of the three Bradley daughters on *Petticoat Junction*?

9) Besides his moose strength, what was Bullwinkle's great talent?

10) What character did Patrick Macnee portray on *The Avengers*?

Quiz 17 Answers

1) Alexander Waverly

2) Stalag 13

3) Ann Marie

4) 1997

5) Tom and Dick

6) Pottsylvania

7) President of a toy manufacturing company

8) Betty Jo, Bobbie Jo, Billie Jo

9) He could remember everything he ever ate.

10) Jonathan Steed

Quiz 18

1) What was the name of the van the group was always driving on the cartoon *Scooby Doo, Where Are You?*

2) Bugs Bunny often finds himself at the wrong end of a gun usually toted by what two characters?

3) Who played the two American intelligence agents on *I Spy*?

4) What was the occupation of Steven Douglas on *My Three Sons*?

5) To prevent continuity problems and allow the episodes to be shown in any order, which 1960s sitcom was always set during winter?

6) Where did Rocky and Bullwinkle live?

7) What were the first names of the four stars of *The Monkees?*

8) On *The Saint*, what was the real name of the character played by Roger Moore?

9) On *The Flying Nun*, what was Sally Field's character name?

10) On *Star Trek*, who played Ensign Chekov?

Quiz 18 Answers

1) Mystery Machine
2) Elmer Fudd and Yosemite Sam
3) Robert Culp and Bill Cosby
4) Aeronautical engineer
5) *Hogan's Heroes* (1965–1971)
6) Frostbite Falls, Minnesota
7) Davy, Micky, Mike, Peter
8) Simon Templar
9) Sister Betrille
10) Walter Koenig

Quiz 19

1) Who was the creator of *The Dick Van Dyke Show* and appeared on the show in a supporting role?

2) On *Star Trek*, what was the name of Spock's father?

3) Who was the director of the St. Louis Zoo and co-host of *Mutual of Omaha's Wild Kingdom?*

4) Who was Dick Dastardly's pet?

5) Where did Rocky and Bullwinkle play college football?

6) James MacArthur, Danny Williams on *Hawaii Five-O*, was the adopted son of what famous actress?

7) What were the names of the four teenagers who joined Scooby-Doo on the cartoon *Scooby Doo, Where Are You?*

8) What was the name of the torpedo boat on *McHale's Navy?*

9) Lucille Ball played her brother-in-law's secretary in what kind of business on *Here's Lucy?*

10) What movie was used as a model for *I Dream of Jeannie?*

Quiz 19 Answers

1) Carl Reiner – He appeared as Alan Brady on the show.
2) Sarek
3) Marlin Perkins
4) Muttley
5) Wossamotta U
6) Helen Hayes
7) Fred, Daphne, Velma, Shaggy
8) *PT-73*
9) Employment agency
10) *The Brass Bottle* (1964) – In the movie, Tony Randall unleashes a genie played by Burl Ives; Barbara Eden played Randall's girlfriend.

Quiz 20

1) What was the name of the recurring criminal nemesis of Steve McGarrett on *Hawaii Five-O*?
2) What sitcom star was the son of a famous conductor?
3) What British show had the opening line "I am not a number! I am a free man!"?
4) On the cartoon, what was the name of the Jetson's dog?
5) What two actors played the lead roles on *Adam-12*?
6) What was the name of Dudley Do-Right's horse?
7) What series featured Tod and Buz, two young drifters?
8) In what town were *Petticoat Junction* and *Green Acres* set?
9) Besides the two hosts, what actor appeared in the most *Rowan & Martin's Laugh-In* episodes?
10) What sitcom character's real name was Exigius 12½?

Quiz 20 Answers

1) Wo Fat
2) Werner Klemperer who played Colonel Klink on *Hogan's Heroes* was the son of famed conductor Otto Klemperer.
3) *The Prisoner* (1967–1968)
4) Astro
5) Martin Milner and Kent McCord
6) Horse
7) *Route 66* (1960–1964)

8) Hooterville
9) Ruth Buzzi - She appeared in all the episodes.
10) Uncle Martin, the Martian on *My Favorite Martian*

Quiz 21

1) What was the name of the robot on *Lost in Space*?
2) How many points did Bullwinkle have on his antlers?
3) In the opening credits for the first season of *Gilligan's Island*, the U.S. flag was at half-mast as the *Minnow* pulls out of harbor; why was the flag at half-mast?
4) What was the name of the character played by Joe Flynn on *McHale's Navy*?
5) The theme music for *Monty Python's Flying Circus* was written by what composer?
6) What were the full character names of the two roles played by Patty Duke on *The Patty Duke Show*?
7) On *The Flintstones*, what fraternal order did Fred and Barney belong to?
8) What was the last name of the family on *Hazel*?
9) What was the daughter's first name on *The Addams Family*?
10) Who played the title role on *The Farmer's Daughter* which was based on a 1947 Loretta Young movie of the same name?

Quiz 21 Answers

1) Robot
2) Six – three on each side
3) John F. Kennedy's assassination – The scene was filmed in November 1963 in Hawaii; the cast and crew learned of Kennedy's assassination on the last day of filming.
4) Captain Binghamton
5) John Philip Sousa – "The Liberty Bell March"
6) Patty Lane and Cathy Lane
7) Water Buffaloes
8) Baxter
9) Wednesday
10) Inger Stevens

Quiz 22

1) Howard McNear played what famous sitcom supporting character?
2) What future Oscar winner was a bikini clad go-go dancer on *Rowan & Martin's Laugh-In*?
3) What were the first names of Rob and Laura's neighbors on *The Dick Van Dyke Show*?
4) On *The Prisoner*, all the characters are assigned numbers rather than names; what is the number assigned to the title character?
5) What was the name of Morticia's man-eating plant on *The Addams Family*?
6) Who hosted *Night Gallery*?
7) When danger appeared, cartoon character Quick Draw McGraw became what super hero?
8) Who played the title role on the teen series *Gidget*?
9) What city was the police series *Ironside* set in?
10) What series was known for the catchphrase "Missed it by that much"?

Quiz 22 Answers

1) Floyd Lawson – the barber on *The Andy Griffith Show*
2) Goldie Hawn
3) Jerry and Millie
4) Six
5) Cleopatra
6) Rod Serling
7) El Kabong
8) Sally Field
9) San Francisco
10) *Get Smart* (1965–1970)

1970s

Quiz 1

1) Who played the title role on the private eye series *Barnaby Jones*?
2) On *Barney Miller*, what was the number of police station precinct?
3) What was the last name of the building superintendent played by Pat Harrington Jr. on *One Day at a Time*?
4) What actor or actress had the most guest starring roles on *Fantasy Island*?
5) What popular series of short videos included segments like *Interjection!*; *Conjunction Junction*; *Lolly, Lolly, Lolly, Get Your Adverbs Here*; and *I'm Just a Bill*?
6) In *One Day at a Time*, what were the first names of the two daughters?
7) On *Happy Days*, who was the oldest Cunningham child?
8) Who was original choice of the creators of *Columbo* to play the detective?
9) Who played the live-in maid Mildred on *McMillan & Wife*?
10) Who was the original host of the daytime version of *Wheel of Fortune*?

Quiz 1 Answers

1) Buddy Ebsen
2) 12th
3) Schneider
4) Carol Lynley - 11 appearances
5) *Schoolhouse Rock!*
6) Julie and Barbara
7) Chuck – He was phased out.
8) Bing Crosby
9) Nancy Walker
10) Chuck Woolery

Quiz 2

1) What was Hawkeye's full name on *M*A*S*H*?
2) What were the full character names of the title characters on *Laverne & Shirley*?

51

3) How did the two boys come to live with Phillip Drummond on *Diff'rent Strokes*?

4) What was the name of the diner where Alice worked while waiting for her break as a singer on *Alice*?

5) What character did McLean Stevenson play on *M*A*S*H*?

6) *Wonder Woman* was based on the character created by William Moulton Marston who was a psychologist and inventor of what well known device?

7) What was the name of Bill Bixby's character and the Hulk's alter ego on *The Incredible Hulk*?

8) The series *McCloud* was a television adaptation of what Clint Eastwood movie?

9) *Mork and Mindy* was a spinoff from what sitcom?

10) What was the name of the late-night music show hosted by Wolfman Jack?

Quiz 2 Answers

1) Benjamin Franklin Pierce
2) Laverne DeFazio and Shirley Feeney
3) He promised his dying housekeeper that he would take care of her boys.
4) Mel's Diner
5) Henry Blake
6) Lie detector – thus the idea for Wonder Woman's Lasso of Truth
7) Dr. David Banner
8) *Coogan's Bluff* (1968)
9) *Happy Days* (1974–1984)
10) *The Midnight Special* (1972–1981)

Quiz 3

1) What was Lt. Columbo's first name?
2) What series that ran on PBS stations followed the lives of the Bellamy family and their servants?
3) On *The New Dick Van Dyke Show*, who played Dick Van Dyke's wife?
4) What was the name of the brewery where the girls worked on *Laverne & Shirley*?
5) What were the first names of the mother and father on *Good Times*?
6) What was Archie's nickname for Edith on *All in the Family*?
7) What was the occupation of Tom, the father, on *Eight Is Enough*?

8) On the show *Chico and the Man*, Freddie Prinze played Chico; who played the man?

9) What was the name of Andy Kaufman's character on *Taxi*?

10) What clothing term did Catherine Bach originate based on her role on *The Dukes of Hazzard*?

Quiz 3 Answers

1) Frank – It was never said during the series but showed up on an ID badge in one episode. The series was never created with the idea that he had a first name.

2) *Upstairs Downstairs* (1971–1975)

3) Hope Lange

4) Shotz Brewery

5) Florida and James

6) Dingbat

7) Columnist for a Sacramento, California newspaper

8) Jack Albertson

9) Latka Gravas

10) Daisy Dukes – extremely short, form-fitting, denim cut-off shorts

Quiz 4

1) What show featured the character Sgt. Pepper Anderson?

2) DIY show *This Old House* debuted in 1979; who was the original master carpenter on the show?

3) One of the actors on *The Jeffersons* helped Norman Lear create a show based on his own life; what was the show?

4) What children's series featured live action films from several countries and was hosted by Kukla, Fran, and Ollie?

5) What series based on a novel of the same name was about the adventures of the staff of a country veterinary office in 1940s Yorkshire England?

6) What city was the setting for *Happy Days*?

7) What mountains did the Walton family live in on *The Waltons*?

8) Jamie Sommers on *The Bionic Woman* became bionic as a result of what?

9) Lani O'Grady who played the daughter Mary on *Eight Is Enough* was the younger sister of Don Grady who played a son on a very popular 1960s sitcom; what was the show?

10) What was the name of Fred's beloved dead wife on *Sanford and Son*?

Quiz 4 Answers

1) *Police Woman* (1974–1978) – starring Angie Dickinson
2) Norm Abram
3) *Good Times* – The Michael Evans character on *Good Times* was based on the early life of actor Mike Evans who played Lionel on *The Jeffersons*.
4) *CBS Children's Film Festival*
5) *All Creatures Great and Small* (1978–1990)
6) Milwaukee, Wisconsin
7) Blue Ridge Mountains – Virginia
8) Skydiving accident
9) *My Three Sons* – He played Robbie Douglas.
10) Elizabeth

Quiz 5

1) What was the name of the central family on the popular miniseries *Rich Man, Poor Man*?
2) What was the make and model of Rockford's car on *The Rockford Files*?
3) What was the name of Ricardo Montalban's character on *Fantasy Island*?
4) What comedy variety show became a hit with phrases like "The devil made me do it!"?
5) On *Buck Rogers in the 25th Century*, what was the empire the Earth is battling?
6) What drama series was a spinoff of *The Mary Tyler Moore Show*?
7) What sports drama was named after the high school sports nickname of its lead actor?
8) What series was a remake of the British show *Steptoe and Son*?
9) Fred Grandy played Gopher Smith on *The Love Boat*; what was Gopher's job on the ship?
10) What series was based on the 1970s British show *Man About the House*?

Quiz 5 Answers

1) Jordache
2) Pontiac Firebird
3) Mr. Roarke

4) *The Flip Wilson Show* (1970–1974)
5) Draconian
6) *Lou Grant* (1977–1982)
7) *The White Shadow* (1978–1981) – Ken Howard who played Ken Reeves, a former professional basketball player and high school basketball coach, was given the nickname "The White Shadow" by the Long Island, New York press in 1961 when at age 17, he was the only white starter on the Manhasset High School varsity basketball team.
8) *Sanford and Son* (1972–1977)
9) Purser
10) *Three's Company* (1976–1984)

Quiz 6

1) What three shows rotated on the original *Sunday NBC Mystery Movie?*
2) What police drama featured two Oscar winners in its lead roles?
3) What drama starred Leo McKern as a portly eccentric London criminal law barrister?
4) What sitcom was a spinoff from *Soap?*
5) What were the first names of the three buddies growing up in Los Angeles on *What's Happening!!?*
6) Who played the title role on the undercover cop series *Baretta?*
7) Who played the title role on *Trapper John, M.D.?*
8) What sitcom was based on a 1978 Walter Matthau and Glenda Jackson film of the same name?
9) What town was the setting for *Little House on the Prairie?*
10) How did the name Muppet originate for the characters on *The Muppet Show?*

Quiz 6 Answers

1) *McCloud, Columbo, McMillan & Wife*
2) *The Streets of San Francisco* (1972–1977) – starring Karl Malden and Michael Douglas
3) *Rumpole of the Bailey* (1978–1992)
4) *Benson* (1979–1986) – starring Robert Guillaume
5) Roger, Rerun, Dwayne
6) Robert Blake
7) Pernell Roberts
8) *House Calls* (1979–1982) – starring Wayne Rogers and Lynn

Redgrave
9) Walnut Grove, Minnesota
10) It is a combination of marionette and puppet.

Quiz 7

1) Who played the role of the young Reverend Fordwick on *The Waltons*?
2) Charlotte Rae's character on *Diff'rent Strokes* was spun off to what series?
3) Who played the title role on *Quincy M.E.*?
4) Who played the two brothers and title characters of the miniseries *Rich Man, Poor Man*?
5) What was Felix Unger's occupation on *The Odd Couple*?
6) Who played Myrna Turner, Oscar Madison's secretary, on *The Odd Couple*?
7) What series had a character with the full name Juan Luis Pedro Felipo De Huevos Epstein?
8) Who played Detective Phil Fish on *Barney Miller*?
9) What city was *Alice* set in?
10) What was the daily primetime satirical soap opera set in Fernwood, Ohio and starring Louise Lasser in the title role as a housewife struggling to cope with the increasingly bizarre and violent events around her?

Quiz 7 Answers

1) John Ritter
2) *The Facts of Life* (1979-1988)
3) Jack Klugman
4) Peter Strauss and Nick Nolte
5) Photographer
6) Penny Marshall
7) *Welcome Back, Kotter* (1975-1979) - Juan Epstein played by Robert Hegyes
8) Abe Vogoda
9) Phoenix, Arizona
10) *Mary Hartman Mary Hartman* (1976-1977)

Quiz 8

1) What were the names of the Ewing couple who starred on *Knots Landing*?
2) Who played the young Kunta Kinte on the miniseries *Roots*?
3) What were the character first names of the original *Charlie's Angels*?
4) On *McCloud*, Marshal Sam McCloud was temporarily assigned to duty in New York City; where was he from?
5) What was the name of the sheriff on *The Dukes of Hazzard*?
6) What was the character name of the salesman who always wears tacky suits on *WKRP in Cincinnati*?
7) What was Billy Crystal's character name on *Soap*?
8) Which of the detectives on *Barney Miller* was also a writer?
9) Who played Mork and Mindy's offspring on *Mork & Mindy*?
10) What science fiction series was set in a futuristic society where reaching the age of 30 was a death sentence?

Quiz 8 Answers

1) Gary and Valene Ewing – played by Ted Shackelford and Joan Van Ark
2) Levar Burton
3) Sabrina, Kelly, Jill
4) Taos, New Mexico
5) Rosco P. Coltrane
6) Herb Tarlek
7) Jodie Dallas
8) Detective Ron Harris
9) Jonathan Winters
10) *Logan's Run* (1977–1978)

Quiz 9

1) What series followed police officers Mike Danko, Willie Gillis, and Terry Webster?
2) What were the names of the two main families on *Dallas*?
3) What character's catchphrase was "Who loves ya, baby?"
4) *Roots* was based on the family history of what author?
5) Who was the only main cast member to be in both the move and television versions of *M*A*S*H*?

6) The revamped *The Price Is Right* debuted in 1972 with Bob Barker as host; who was the announcer for many years and popularized the "Come on down!" catchphrase?
7) What was the name of the family on *Eight is Enough*?
8) What was the name of the character played by Richard Anderson that Steve Austin worked for on *The Six Million Dollar Man*?
9) What were the first names of the five Partridge children on *The Partridge Family*?
10) What were the first names of the ventriloquist and his dummy on *Soap*?

Quiz 9 Answers

1) *The Rookies* (1972–1976)
2) Ewing and Barnes
3) Kojak
4) Alex Haley
5) Gary Burghoff – Radar O'Reilly
6) Johnny Olson
7) Bradford
8) Oscar Goldman
9) Keith, Laurie, Danny, Tracy, Chris
10) Chuck and Bob

Quiz 10

1) What sitcom featured a never seen character Carlton the doorman?
2) What was the name of Bob Newhart's next-door neighbor played by Bill Daily on *The Bob Newhart Show*?
3) What drama series featured Meredith Baxter and Kristy McNichol as sisters?
4) What drama starred Claude Akins and Frank Converse as a pair of truckers teaming up to haul cargo across the country?
5) On *Shazam!*, a young boy can transform into the superhero Captain Marvel and travels the country fighting evil and helping people; what is the name of the young boy who becomes Captain Marvel?
6) What two actors played the title roles on *Starsky and Hutch*?
7) What is Bob and Emily's last name on *The Bob Newhart Show*?
8) What drama starred Glenn Ford and Julie Harris as a reverend and his wife and family struggling to survive the Great Depression in Tennessee?

9) Who played the title role on *Buck Rogers in the 25th Century?*
10) What comedy show starred Joe Flaherty, Eugene Levy, Andrea Martin, Dave Thomas, John Candy, Catherine O'Hara, Harald Ramis, and Rick Moranis?

Quiz 10 Answers

1) *Rhoda* (1974–1978)
2) Howard Borden
3) *Family* (1976–1980)
4) *Movin' On* (1974–1976)
5) Billy Batson
6) David Soul and Paul Michael Glaser
7) Hartley
8) *The Family Holvak*
9) Gil Gerard
10) *SCTV* (1976–1981)

Quiz 11

1) Who played Maude's daughter Carol on *Maude?*
2) What was the name of the piano playing dog on *The Muppet Show?*
3) Who was the creator and narrator of *The Waltons?*
4) What was Archie Bunker's son-in-law's full name on *All in the Family?*
5) What action adventure comedy starred Roger Moore as English Lord Brett Sinclair and Tony Curtis as American Danny Wilde who are both wealthy playboys and team up to investigate crimes the police can't solve?
6) On *Mork & Mindy,* what planet was Mork from?
7) Who played the title roles on *McMillan & Wife?*
8) *Good Times* was a spinoff from what show?
9) How many different actors on *The Mary Tyler Moore Show* won Emmys?
10) What was George and Louise's only child's name on *The Jeffersons?*

Quiz 11 Answers

1) Adrienne Barbeau
2) Rowlf
3) Earl Hamner Jr.

4) Michael Stivic
5) *The Persuaders!* (1971–1972)
6) Ork
7) Rock Hudson and Susan Saint James
8) *Maude*
9) Six – Mary Tyler Moore, Ted Knight, Betty White, Cloris Leachman, Ed Asner, Valerie Harper
10) Lionel

Quiz 12

1) Based on a movie of the same name, what sitcom was about the misadventures of a WWII U.S. submarine that takes on a group of female nurses.?
2) What series starred Robert Conrad as U.S. Major Gregory "Pappy" Boyington who was squadron leader of a group of fighter pilots stationed on a Pacific island during WWII?
3) On *The Mary Tyler Moore Show*, what are the call letters of the television station where they work?
4) What are the only three characters on *M*A*S*H* to appear in the movie and all the way through the entire television series?
5) Before she became bionic, what was Jamie Sommers occupation on *The Bionic Woman*?
6) What was the name of the cruise ship on *The Love Boat*?
7) Who was the name of the oldest child on *Eight Is Enough*?
8) Who played detective Frank Cannon?
9) Martin Caldin, a U.S. Air Force pilot and NASA public relations person, wrote the novel *Cyborg* which was the source material for what series?
10) At the end of *M*A*S*H*, what character stayed in Korea?

Quiz 12 Answers

1) *Operation Petticoat* (1977–1979)
2) *Black Sheep Squadron* (1976–1978)
3) WJM-TV
4) Hawkeye, Margaret, Father Mulcahy
5) Professional tennis player
6) *Pacific Princess*
7) David
8) William Conrad

9) *The Six Million Dollar Man* (1974–1978)
10) Maxwell Klinger

Quiz 13

1) Who played the title role on *Ellery Queen*?
2) Who played the title role on *Benson*?
3) Who played the title roles on *Nanny and the Professor*?
4) What was the name of Baretta's pet cockatoo on *Baretta*?
5) Who played the title role on *McCloud*?
6) What was the character name of the Spanish waiter on *Fawlty Towers*?
7) What sitcom star who came to fame in the 1970s has highly superior autobiographical memory, a rare condition also known as hyperthymesia or total recall memory where the person can remember specific details of virtually every day of their life?
8) What was John Cleese's full character name on *Fawlty Towers*?
9) What was the name of Robert Urich's private eye character on *Vega$*?
10) What was the character name of Rockford's lawyer on *The Rockford Files*?

Quiz 13 Answers

1) Jim Hutton
2) Robert Guillaume
3) Juliet Mills and Richard Long
4) Fred
5) Dennis Weaver
6) Manuel
7) Marilu Henner – star on *Taxi*
8) Basil Fawlty
9) Dan Tanna
10) Beth Davenport

Quiz 14

1) What was the name of Sonny and Cher's first series?
2) The *Donny and Marie* variety show featured the entire Osmond family; how many siblings were there in total?
3) What was the name of the character Betty White played on *The*

Mary Tyler Moore Show?

4) Before *Three's Company*, John Ritter played a minister on what 1970s drama?
5) What were the names of the two characters that heckle the rest of the cast from the balcony on *The Muppet Show*?
6) Who played the commander of *Battlestar Galactica*?
7) What actor played Dr. Jerry Robinson on *The Bob Newhart Show* and went on to become an award-winning director of hundreds of television episodes for a variety of shows?
8) Keith Moon of The Who was the inspiration for which of the Muppets on *The Muppet Show*?
9) What western starred Peter Duel and Ben Murphy as Hannibal Hayes and Kid Curry, two of the most wanted outlaws in the history of the West, who are seeking amnesty?
10) What was the name of the groundbreaking 26-part documentary series about WWII narrated by Laurence Olivier?

Quiz 14 Answers

1) *The Sonny and Cher Comedy Hour* (1971–1974)
2) Nine – Virl, Tom, Alan, Wayne, Merrill, Jay, Donny, Marie, Jimmy
3) Sue Ann Nivens
4) *The Waltons* (1971–1981)
5) Statler and Waldorf
6) Lorne Greene
7) Peter Bonerz
8) Animal – the drummer
9) *Alias Smith and Jones* (1971–1973)
10) *The World at War* (1973–1976)

Quiz 15

1) What series was loosely based on the novel and movie *Spencer's Mountain* staring Henry Fonda and Maureen O'Hara?
2) What was the name of the character Howard Hesseman played on *WKRP in Cincinnati*?
3) Cloris Leachman starred in a spinoff from *The Mary Tyler Moore Show*; what was the name of the character she played?
4) Who played the title role on *Maude*?
5) On *Kung Fu*, what was Master Po's name for young Cain?
6) How many children were there in the Walton family on *The*

Waltons?

7) What city was Mork & Mindy set in?

8) What Jack Webb series starred a real-life husband and wife Julie London and Bobby Troup?

9) What sitcom starred Donna Pescow as a middle class Italian-American who marries into a wealthy family?

10) What daytime soap opera is set in Genoa City and tells the story of the Abbott and Newman families?

Quiz 15 Answers

1) *The Waltons* - Earl Hamner Jr. wrote the book and movie script and created *The Waltons*.

2) Dr. Johnny Fever

3) Phyllis Lindstrom

4) Bea Arthur

5) Grasshopper

6) Seven - John-Boy, Jason, Ben, Jim-Bob, Mary Ellen, Erin, Elizabeth

7) Boulder, Colorado

8) *Emergency!* (1972-1979)

9) *Angie* (1979-1980)

10) *The Young and the Restless* - debuted in 1973

Quiz 16

1) What series was part of the *NBC Wednesday Mystery Movie* rotation and starred George Peppard as a suave, Polish-American freelance investigator who solved seemingly impossible thefts?

2) On *The Jeffersons*, what was George's business?

3) What was the name of the island Wonder Woman was from?

4) What was the name of the Ewing ranch on *Dallas*?

5) Who was the head news writer on *The Mary Tyler Moore Show*?

6) Who were the original co-hosts of *Good Morning America* when it debuted in 1975?

7) What was the name of the police informant played by Antonio Fargas on *Starsky and Hutch*?

8) On *Battlestar Galactica*, who played the Imperious Leader of the enemy race?

9) What science fiction comedy starred Richard Benjamin as Adam Quark, captain of an outer space garbage collector ship?

10) Who played the title roles on *The Ropers*?

Quiz 16 Answers

1) *Banacek* (1972–1974)
2) Dry cleaning
3) Paradise Island
4) Southfork
5) Murray Slaughter
6) David Hartman and Nancy Dussault
7) Huggy Bear
8) Patrick Macnee
9) *Quark* (1977–1978)
10) Norman Fell and Audra Lindley

Quiz 17

1) What series was a continuation of *All in the Family* rather than a spinoff?
2) What was the last name of the family on *Good Times*?
3) On *Kojak*, what was Kojak's first name?
4) What children's series had a family who were thrown back in time and must survive in the age of dinosaurs?
5) On *Chico and the Man*, what was the business the lead characters worked in?
6) On *Battlestar Galactica*, what was the name of the enemy race?
7) What author wrote the series of books on which *Little House on the Prairie* was based?
8) Who was the only angel to last the entire series on *Charlie's Angels*?
9) On *Kung Fu*, what was the name of David Carradine's character?
10) Who starred in the title role as the lone survivor of the legendary sunken continent of Atlantis on *Man from Atlantis*?

Quiz 17 Answers

1) *Archie Bunker's Place* (1979–1983)
2) Evans
3) Theo
4) *Land of the Lost* (1974–1977)
5) Mechanic's garage
6) Cylons
7) Laura Ingalls Wilder

8) Kelly Garrett – played by Jaclyn Smith
9) Kwai Chang Caine
10) Patrick Duffy

Quiz 18

1) *Happy Days* was a spinoff from what show?
2) Who played the globe-trotting amateur detectives Jonathan and Jennifer Hart on *Hart to Hart*?
3) David Carradine's character on *Kung Fu* had been trained as what?
4) Who played Rhoda's sister Brenda on *Rhoda*?
5) On *M*A*S*H*, what was Radar's favorite drink?
6) What sitcom starred Meredith Baxter and David Birney as two struggling newlyweds, a rich Catholic and a Jewish cabbie?
7) What was Mary's last name on *The Mary Tyler Moore Show*?
8) Who starred as Carl Kolchak, a Chicago reporter who always got into situations involving the supernatural on *Kolchak: The Night Stalker*?
9) What was the number of the mobile hospital unit on *M*A*S*H*?
10) What brand was Lt. Columbo's car?

Quiz 18 Answers

1) *Love American Style* – There was a segment called "Love and the Happy Days" with the same characters and premise.
2) Robert Wagner and Stefanie Powers
3) Shaolin Monk
4) Julie Kavner
5) Grape Nehi
6) *Bridget Loves Bernie* (1972–1973)
7) Richards
8) Darren McGavin
9) 4077
10) Peugeot

Quiz 19

1) What actor was the narrator and uncredited voice for the Hulk on *The Incredible Hulk* and had a famous role on a 1960s sitcom?
2) Created as a female counterpart to Captain Marvel, what series featured an archaeologist who finds an amulet that allows her to

transform into a superheroine goddess and fight evil?

3) What was the name of John Travolta's character on *Welcome Back, Kotter*?

4) What science fiction series starred Martin Landau as commander of the crew of Moonbase Alpha who must struggle to survive when a massive explosion throws the moon into deep space?

5) What parts of Jamie Sommers' body were bionic on *The Bionic Woman*?

6) What newsmagazine debuted in 1978 as ABC's answer to *60 Minutes*?

7) What was the name of Christopher Lloyd's character on *Taxi*?

8) What children's show starred Morgan Freeman, Rita Moreno, Mel Brooks, and Zero Mostel?

9) *The Partridge Family* was based on what real-life musical family?

10) What series starred Burt Reynolds as a homicide detective in his hometown of Santa Luisa, California?

Quiz 19 Answers

1) Ted Cassidy – He played Lurch on *The Addams Family*.
2) *Isis* (1975–1976)
3) Vinnie Barbarino
4) *Space: 1999* (1975–1977)
5) Both legs, one arm, one ear
6) *20/20*
7) Jim Ignatowski
8) *The Electric Company* (1971–1977) – The show was targeted at children 7-10 years old and was designed to teach basic reading concepts through skits, cartoons, vignettes, and regular features.
9) The Cowsills – They were considered for the show, but the children were older than the parts written for the series.
10) *Dan August* (1970–1971)

Quiz 20

1) Who was the original host of the music and dance show *Soul Train*?
2) What did Lieutenant Kojak often have in his mouth on *Kojak*?
3) What make and model of car was the General Lee on *The Dukes of Hazzard*?
4) What drama series featured the joys and heartaches of the Lawrence family of Pasadena, California?

5) What historical drama was broadcast on PBS Masterpiece Theatre and featured a British officer returning home to Cornwall after the American Revolutionary War to right wrongs and reunite with the love of his life?

6) What was the first name of the son on *Sanford and Son*?

7) What actor appeared the most times as the murderer on *Columbo*?

8) What work did Laverne and Shirley do at the brewery on *Laverne & Shirley*?

9) Who were the only two actors on *The Partridge Family* who sang on any recordings?

10) What actress played Flo in the movie *Alice Doesn't Live Here Anymore* and played Belle on the series *Alice* which was based on the movie?

Quiz 20 Answers

1) Don Cornelius
2) Lollipop
3) Dodge Charger
4) *Family* (1976–1980)
5) *Poldark* (1975–1977)
6) Lamont
7) Patrick McGoohan – four times
8) Bottle cappers
9) Shirley Jones and David Cassidy
10) Diane Ladd

Quiz 21

1) What science documentary series debuted in 1974?

2) What comedy adventure starred Greg Evigan as a trucker who along with his pet chimpanzee traveled the highways of America?

3) What series was an American version of the British sitcom *Please Sir*?

4) What was Dennis Becker's nickname for Rockford on *The Rockford Files*?

5) Who sang the theme song and was the narrator on *The Dukes of Hazzard*?

6) What was the name of the company that the *Taxi* characters worked for?

7) What *Dallas* spinoff was set in a coastal suburb of Los Angeles?

8) Who starred in the title role of *The Life and Times of Grizzly Adams*

about a falsely accused man who must flee into the mountains?
9) What western series starred Richard Boone as an ex-gunfighter who uses contemporary methods of solving crimes?
10) *Maude* was a spinoff from *All in the Family*; what was Maude's relationship to the Bunkers?

Quiz 21 Answers

1) *Nova*
2) *B.J. and the Bear* (1978–1981)
3) *Welcome Back, Kotter* (1975–1979)
4) Jimbo
5) Waylon Jennings
6) Sunshine Cab
7) *Knots Landing* (1979–1993)
8) Dan Haggerty
9) *Hec Ramsey* (1972–1974)
10) She was Edith's cousin.

1980s

Quiz 1

1) What series featured a retired intelligence agent turned private detective who helped people in need?
2) On *Falcon Crest*, what was the name of the family that owned the Falcon Crest Winery?
3) What was the name of the children's reading series hosted by LeVar Burton?
4) What were the first names of the title characters on *Cagney & Lacey*?
5) What was the name of Norm's wife on *Cheers*?
6) In what city did *The Oprah Winfrey Show* originate?
7) Which character on *The Golden Girls* appeared on six different sitcoms?
8) What talent show was originally hosted by Ed McMahon?
9) Who played the title characters on *Scarecrow and Mrs. King*?
10) What is cartoon cat Garfield's favorite food?

Quiz 1 Answers

1) *The Equalizer* (1985–1989)
2) Gioberti
3) *Reading Rainbow* – debuted 1983
4) Christine Cagney and Mary Beth Lacey
5) Vera
6) Chicago
7) Sophia – Estelle Getty played Sophia on *The Golden Girls*, *The Golden Palace*, *Empty Nest*, *Blossom*, *Nurses*, and *Ladies Man*.
8) *Star Search* (1983–2004)
9) Bruce Boxleitner and Kate Jackson
10) Lasagna

Quiz 2

1) On *The Wonder Years*, one of the child actors went on to get a bachelor's degree in mathematics and wrote several books on math; which character did they play?
2) What were the first names of the mother and father played by Phylicia Rashad and Bill Cosby on *The Cosby Show*?

3) What series starred Bruce Willis in a detective agency?
4) What were the three main competing syndicated newsmagazine shows that all debuted in the late 1980s?
5) What was the occupation of Richard Mulligan's character on *Empty Nest*?
6) One of Johnny Depp's early starring roles was on what police show?
7) What sitcom followed the lives of the residents of a Washington D.C. apartment building?
8) Who was the musical director on *Late Night with David Letterman*?
9) Between the two leads, what series had the Best Actress in a Drama Series Emmy winner six straight years?
10) Who played the title roles as private eye brothers on *Simon & Simon*?

Quiz 2 Answers

1) Winnie Cooper – played by Danica McKellar
2) Clair and Heathcliff
3) *Moonlighting* (1985–1989)
4) *A Current Affair* (1986), *Inside Edition* (1988), *Hard Copy* (1989)
5) Pediatrician
6) *21 Jump Street* (1987–1991)
7) *227* (1985–1990)
8) Paul Shaffer
9) *Cagney & Lacey* (1981–1988)
10) Jameson Parker and Gerald McRaney

Quiz 3

1) What series had the opening "He awoke and found himself trapped in the past, facing mirror images that were not his own, and driven by an unknown force to change history for the better"?
2) Alan Thicke played Jason Seaver on *Growing Pains*; what was his character's occupation?
3) Who played the dads on the sitcom *My Two Dads*?
4) What series featured three Vietnam War veterans working as private detectives using their helicopter in southern California?
5) What was the name of the college on *A Different World*?
6) What was the captain's name on *Star Trek: The Next Generation*?
7) On *Seinfeld*, what was Kramer's first name?
8) What is grandpa Simpson's first name on *The Simpsons*?

9) What show featured four actresses who all won Emmys for their roles during the run of the series?

10) Who played the title role on the sitcom *Major Dad?*

Quiz 3 Answers

1) *Quantum Leap* (1989–1993)
2) Psychologist
3) Paul Reiser and Greg Evigan
4) *Riptide* (1984–1986)
5) Hillman
6) Captain Jean-Luc Picard
7) Cosmo
8) Abraham
9) *The Golden Girls* (1985–1992)
10) Gerald McRaney

Quiz 4

1) What sitcom featured Tom Hanks in drag?
2) In what city was *Matlock* set?
3) Who was a co-host and correspondent on *Entertainment Tonight* for 29 years?
4) Who played the Beast on *Beauty and the Beast?*
5) Who was the host of *Rescue 911* featuring reenactments of 911 emergency situations?
6) Who played Grace Van Owen on *L.A. Law* and starred in a popular 1970s sitcom?
7) In the sitcom *Married with Children*, what was the dog's name?
8) Who played the title role on *Punky Brewster?*
9) What was the name of *The Cosby Show* spinoff?
10) What were the first names of the four *Designing Women?*

Quiz 4 Answers

1) *Bosom Buddies* (1980–1982)
2) Atlanta
3) Mary Hart
4) Ron Perlman
5) William Shatner
6) Susan Dey – She also appeared on *The Partridge Family.*

7) Buck
8) Soleil Moon Frye
9) *A Different World* (1987–1993)
10) Julia, Suzanne, Mary Jo, Charlene

Quiz 5

1) What was the nickname that the Dwight Schultz character was known as on *The A-Team*?
2) What series was about a young girl who was abandoned with her dog in a shopping center and is eventually adopted by an elderly widower?
3) What drama series finale called into question the reality of the entire series?
4) Who played Captain Frank Furillo on *Hill Street Blues*?
5) What series featured nurses and doctors in a Vietnam War field hospital?
6) Who provided the voice of the car on *Knight Rider*?
7) What city was the setting for *Dynasty*?
8) What twins played the role of *Michelle* on Full House?
9) Who played detective Virgil Tibbs on the series *In the Heat of the Night*?
10) Every episode of *Seinfeld* contains an image or reference to what superhero?

Quiz 5 Answers

1) "Howling Mad" Murdock
2) *Punky Brewster* (1984–1988)
3) *St. Elsewhere* (1982–1988) – The final episode showed that the hospital was inside the snow globe of autistic Tommy Westphall, and everything that had happened was his imagination.
4) Daniel J. Travanti
5) *China Beach* (1988–1991)
6) William Daniels – also starred in *St. Elsewhere* and *Boy Meets World*
7) Denver, Colorado
8) Mary-Kate and Ashley Olsen
9) Howard E. Rollins Jr.
10) Superman

Quiz 6

1) What series had a female private detective who invented a fictitious male boss?
2) Who played Balki Bartokomous on the sitcom *Perfect Strangers*?
3) Who is the voice of Marge on *The Simpsons*?
4) What sitcom had a very famous dream sequence series finale?
5) What sitcom starred Ricky Schroeder as spoiled rich kid Ricky Stratton?
6) Who played Whitley Gilbert on *A Different World*?
7) Who played the role of Jackie Harris on *Roseanne*?
8) Judge Harry T. Stone on *Night Court* was a huge fan of what singer?
9) What was the name of the all-female building where the characters lived on *Bosom Buddies*?
10) Who was Alex's youngest sibling on *Family Ties*?

Quiz 6 Answers

1) *Remington Steele* (1982-1987)
2) Bronson Pinchot
3) Julie Kavner
4) *Newhart* - In the final episode, the entire series is revealed to be a dream of Robert Hartley, Bob Newhart's character from his previous series *The Bob Newhart Show*.
5) *Silver Spoons* (1982-1987)
6) Jasmine Guy
7) Laurie Metcalf
8) Mel Torme
9) Susan B. Anthony Hotel
10) Andy – He was born during the series run.

Quiz 7

1) On *Who's the Boss*, what was Tony's occupation before becoming a housekeeper?
2) Who played the role of Nell Harper on *Gimme a Break!*?
3) What syndicated newsmagazine had David Frost and Bill O'Reilly as its first two hosts?
4) Who played the synthetic life form, Lt. Commander Data, on *Star Trek: The Next Generation*?
5) Who played the title role in the private eye series *Remington Steele*?

6) What was Doogie's best friend's first name on *Doogie Howser, M.D.*?

7) What town was the setting for *Murder, She Wrote*?

8) What office place sitcom was based on a movie of the same name and starred the sister of one of the movie's stars?

9) Who reprised her role as Captain Doreen Lewis from the movie *Private Benjamin* on the series of the same name?

10) What was the name of the hospital on *St. Elsewhere*?

Quiz 7 Answers

1) Baseball player

2) Nell Carter

3) *Inside Edition* – debuted 1988

4) Brent Spiner

5) Pierce Brosnan

6) Vinnie

7) Cabot Cove, Maine

8) *9 to 5* – Rachel Dennison who is Dolly Parton's sister played the role of Doralee that Parton played in the movie.

9) Eileen Brennan

10) St. Eligius

Quiz 8

1) Who played the title role on the crime drama *Hunter*?

2) What series had a teacher as a superhero using a special alien suit?

3) What was the name of the television show Bob Newhart's character hosted on *Newhart*?

4) What was the name of the detective agency on *Moonlighting*?

5) Who played the title roles on the sitcom *Kate & Allie*?

6) What sitcom centered on a church deacon and his assistant who disagreed on what was best for their congregation?

7) What show had John Davidson, Fran Tarkenton, and Cathy Lee Crosby as hosts?

8) Who played Admiral Al Calavicci who appeared mostly as a hologram on *Quantum Leap*?

9) What actor on *Night Court* won four consecutive Emmys for their role?

10) Who played the barmaid Carla on *Cheers*?

Quiz 8 Answers

1) Fred Dryer
2) *The Greatest American Hero* (1981–1983)
3) *Vermont Today*
4) Blue Moon
5) Susan Saint James and Jane Curtin
6) *Amen* (1986–1991)
7) *That's Incredible!* (1980–1984)
8) Dean Stockwell
9) John Larroquette
10) Rhea Perlman

Quiz 9

1) What was the name of the innkeeper played by Bob Newhart on *Newhart*?
2) Who played the title roles on *Cagney & Lacey*?
3) What sitcom character had 93 secretaries during the series run?
4) Who provided the voice of the unseen Robin Masters on *Magnum, P.I.*?
5) What city was the setting for *Family Ties*?
6) What was the name of the inn on *Newhart*?
7) What was the name of the character played by Angela Lansbury on *Murder, She Wrote*?
8) Who played the narrator and voice of the adult Kevin on *The Wonder Years*?
9) What was the name of the family Alf lives with on *Alf*?
10) What was the name of the character played by Bruce Willis on *Moonlighting*?

Quiz 9 Answers

1) Dick Loudon
2) Sharon Gless and Tyne Daly
3) Murphy Brown – Her inability to get a good secretary or one that could work with her was a running joke.
4) Orson Welles
5) Columbus, Ohio
6) Stratford Inn

7) Jessica Fletcher
8) Daniel Stern
9) Tanner
10) David Addison

Quiz 10

1) What show was about the adventures of a housewife and a spy?
2) What was the name of the character played by John O'Hurley on *Seinfeld* and the name of the catalog he produced?
3) What was the name of the children's series starring Paul Reubens as a childlike character?
4) Who played the daughter, Samantha, on *Who's the Boss?*
5) What planet was the space alien Alf from?
6) On *Growing Pains*, what was the family name?
7) Who played Lt. Martin Castillo, the boss of Don Johnson and Philip Michael Thomas on *Miami Vice?*
8) What sitcom starred a real-life husband and wife, and the husband played a character with the same occupation as he had in real life before acting?
9) What series featured the character Steve Urkel?
10) What was the name of the interior design company the characters work at on *Designing Women?*

Quiz 10 Answers

1) *Scarecrow and Mrs. King* (1983–1987)
2) J. Peterman
3) *Pee-wee's Playhouse* (1986–1991)
4) Alyssa Milano
5) Melmac
6) Seaver
7) Edward James Olmos
8) *Webster* (1983–1989) - Alex Karras and Susan Clark starred and were married in real life; Karras played a football player and was himself a former NFL player with the Detroit Lions.
9) *Family Matters* (1989–1998)
10) Sugarbaker & Associates Interior Design

Quiz 11

1) What was Linda Hamilton's job on *Beauty and the Beast*?
2) What were the first names of the parents on *Family Ties*?
3) What was the Lee Major series about a stuntman who moonlights as a bounty hunter?
4) What series was a continuation of *Three's Company*?
5) What series had a retired judge and his last defendant following up on cases that were dismissed due to technicalities?
6) What was Ted Knight's final series?
7) The opening credits for *Newhart* used outtakes from what Oscar winning 1980s film that was also set in New England?
8) What were the last names of the two central detectives on *Miami Vice*?
9) What Leslie Nielsen sitcom was the basis for the *Naked Gun* movie series?
10) Who played the title role on the sitcom *Webster*?

Quiz 11 Answers

1) Assistant District Attorney
2) Steven and Elyse
3) *The Fall Guy* (1981–1986)
4) Three's a Crowd (1984–1985)
5) *Hardcastle and McCormick* (1983–1986)
6) *Too Close for Comfort* (1980–1987) – He died ending the series.
7) *On Golden Pond* – You can see Henry Fonda and Katharine Hepburn in the car. William Lanteau, who played Chester in the series, was also in *On Golden Pond*.
8) Crockett and Tubbs
9) *Police Squad!* (1982)
10) Emmanuel Lewis

Quiz 12

1) What was the title character's first name on *Matlock*?
2) What was the name of the think tank MacGyver worked for on *MacGyver*?
3) What series shared its title and premise with a 1960s Oscar winning film?
4) What was the real first name of the character Screech on *Saved by*

the Bell?

5) What was the name of the television network the characters worked for on *Murphy Brown?*

6) What long running series featured movie stars such as Jane Wyman, Cliff Robertson, Lana Turner, and Kim Novak?

7) What was the limitation on the main character's time travel on *Quantum Leap?*

8) Who played the title role on the sitcom *Charles in Charge?*

9) *The Simpsons* first debuted as a short on what show?

10) What university was the setting for the sitcom *Coach?*

Quiz 12 Answers

1) Ben
2) Phoenix Foundation
3) *In the Heat of the Night* (1988–1995)
4) Samuel
5) FYI News Network
6) *Falcon Crest* (1981–1990)
7) He could only time travel within his own lifetime.
8) Scott Baio
9) *The Tracey Ullman Show* (1987–1990)
10) Minnesota State

Quiz 13

1) What was the name of the car on *Knight Rider?*

2) On *Highway to Heaven*, what was the name of Michael Landon's probationary angel character?

3) What was the horror anthology series that ended with "The Darkside is always there waiting for us to enter; waiting to enter us. Until next time, try to enjoy the daylight"?

4) What reality series had the theme song "Bad Boys"?

5) Who was the original host for *Unsolved Mysteries* which had re-enactments, interviews and updates, about real mysteries?

6) Who played Higgins on *Magnum, P.I.?*

7) On *The Simpsons*, who are the only characters that are drawn with five fingers?

8) What was the name of the high school on *Saved by the Bell?*

9) What future music superstar appeared on the first season of *Fame?*

10) What show has had Bob Saget, Tom Bergeron, and Alfonso Ribeiro as hosts?

Quiz 13 Answers

1) Kitt – Knight Industries Two Thousand
2) Jonathan Smith
3) *Tales from the Darkside* (1983–1988)
4) *Cops* – debuted 1989
5) Robert Stack
6) John Hillerman
7) God and Jesus – All the other characters have four fingers.
8) Bayside
9) Janet Jackson
10) *America's Funniest Home Videos* – debuted 1989

Quiz 14

1) What drama's title added a word to the Oxford English Dictionary due to popular usage?
2) What sitcom's title character was portrayed as being 5–8 years old during the series run but was played by an actor who was 12–18 years old during the show's run?
3) Where was the series *In the Heat of the Night* set?
4) Of the four main stars on Seinfeld, who was the only one not to win an Emmy for the show?
5) What series was spun off from *The Carol Burnett Show*?
6) What was the name of the café originally run by Kirk Devane and later by Larry, Darryl, and Darryl on *Newhart*?
7) What recurring character on *The Simpsons* is voiced by Kelsey Grammer?
8) What were the names of the five children on *The Cosby Show*?
9) What actress received a Best Lead Actress in a Drama Series Emmy nomination for each of the 12 seasons her show ran but never won?
10) Who played the two former Texas Rangers on a cattle drive on the miniseries *Lonesome Dove*?

Quiz 14 Answers

1) *Thirtysomething* (1987–1991)
2) *Webster* (1983–1989)

3) Sparta, Mississippi
4) Jason Alexander
5) *Mama's Family* (1983–1990)
6) Minuteman Café
7) Sideshow Bob
8) Sondra, Denise, Vanessa, Rudy, Theo
9) Angela Lansbury – *Murder, She Wrote*
10) Robert Duvall and Tommy Lee Jones

Quiz 15

1) What sitcom character liked to eat cats?
2) What was the name of George Peppard's character on *The A-Team*?
3) Who played the title role on *The Equalizer*?
4) Who played the title role on *MacGyver*?
5) What was the real complete name of the character Bull played by Richard Moll on the sitcom *Night Court*?
6) What was *The Golden Girls* spinoff also set in Miami with a widowed father and his two adult daughters?
7) Who provided the voice for the bumbling Inspector Gadget on the animated children's show *Inspector Gadget*?
8) What was the last name of Woody on *Cheers*?
9) *Magnum, P.I.* was originally going to be set in southern California but was moved to Hawaii partly because of some network logistics; what was the network consideration?
10) What does the name Alf stand for on *Alf*?

Quiz 15 Answers

1) Alf
2) Hannibal Smith
3) Edward Woodward
4) Richard Dean Anderson
5) Aristotle Nostradamus Shannon
6) *Empty Nest* (1988–1995)
7) Don Adams
8) Boyd
9) CBS did not want to close its Hawaii production offices when *Hawaii Five-O* ended in 1980, so they moved the *Magnum, P.I.* setting to Hawaii.

10) Alien Life Form

Quiz 16

1) What show was only the third to ever end while still at the top of the Nielsen Ratings?
2) Who was host on the true crime series *America's Most Wanted?*
3) Who played assistant coach Luther Van Dam on *Coach?*
4) Who played Dr. Philip Chandler on *St. Elsewhere?*
5) Who originally played the teacher on the sitcom *Head of the Class?*
6) Who played the title role on *The New Mike Hammer?*
7) What crime drama featured Vinnie Terranova as an undercover agent for the Organized Crime Bureau?
8) What drama series had two real life married couples playing married couples?
9) What series featured Joel the janitor, Tom Servo, and Crow T. Robot watching and commenting on bad movies?
10) On the sitcom *Perfect Strangers*, where was Balki from?

Quiz 16 Answers

1) *Seinfeld* (1989-1998)
2) John Walsh
3) Jerry Van Dyke
4) Denzel Washington
5) Howard Hesseman
6) Stacy Keach
7) *Wiseguy* (1987-2009)
8) *L.A. Law* - Married characters Ann Kelsey and Stuart Markowitz were played by real life married couple Jill Eikenberry and Michael Tucker, and married characters Douglas and Sheila Brackman were played by real life couple Alan Rachins and Joanna Frank.
9) *Mystery Science Theater 3000* (1988-1999)
10) Mypos - small Mediterranean island

Quiz 17

1) What sitcom was known for obliterating the fourth wall to the point of casually chatting with the studio audience and cast members either in or out of character?
2) What were the names of the two feuding families on *Dynasty?*

3) Who played the title role on *Doogie Howser, M.D.*?
4) What did T.J. stand for in *T.J. Hooker*?
5) Who played the role of teacher Lydia Grant on *Fame*?
6) What was the name of the time traveling scientist on *Quantum Leap*?
7) *Simon & Simon* was about private detective brothers; what city was it set in?
8) Who played the role of English ship pilot John Blackthorne on the miniseries *Shogun*?
9) What syndicated late night talk show debuted in 1989?
10) Before starring in *Modern Family*, Ed O'Neill was best known for playing what television dad?

Quiz 17 Answers

1) *It's Garry Shandling's Show* (1986-1990)
2) Carrington and Colby
3) Neil Patrick Harris
4) Thomas Jefferson
5) Debbie Allen
6) Sam Beckett
7) San Diego
8) Richard Chamberlain
9) *The Aresenio Hall Show* (1989-1994)
10) Al Bundy – *Married with Children*

Quiz 18

1) What action comedy starring David Rasche was a parody of the *Dirty Harry* movies?
2) Ringo Starr narrated what children's show?
3) Who played both dirty cop Sal Benedetto and later Lt. Norman Buntz on *Hill Street Blues*?
4) Who was a creator for both *Hill Street Blues* and *L.A. Law*?
5) What was Betty White's character name on *The Golden Girls*?
6) What anthology series was created by Steven Spielberg and featured many famous actors and had episodes directed by Spielberg, Clint Eastwood, Martin Scorsese, and Robert Zemeckis?
7) Who had the title role on *Dear John*, a sitcom about a support group for divorced and widowed people?

8) Who played special agent Bill Maxwell on *The Greatest American Hero*?
9) What was the actual bay referred to in the series title *Baywatch*?
10) After receiving five Emmy awards for her role, what sitcom actress turned down all future nominations for the same role?

Quiz 18 Answers

1) *Sledge Hammer!* (1986–1988)
2) *Thomas the Tank Engine & Friends* – debuted 1984
3) Dennis Franz
4) Steven Bochco
5) Rose Nylund
6) *Amazing Stories* (1985–1987)
7) Judd Hirsch
8) Robert Culp
9) Santa Monica Bay
10) Candice Bergen - *Murphy Brown*

Quiz 19

1) What was the real name of the Beast on *Beauty and the Beast*?
2) On *The Wonder Years*, what was Fred Savage's character name?
3) What sketch comedy starred Dave Foley, Bruce McCulloch, Kevin McDonald, Scott Thompson, and Mark McKinney?
4) What sitcom featured a group of waitresses who worked at a fancy restaurant at the top of a skyscraper?
5) What drama was based on a novel and 1949 film of the same name and detailed the lives of the residents of the sleepy southern town of Truro, Florida?
6) *Family Matters* was a spinoff of what show?
7) What series was revived after being canceled after one season because *Magnum, P.I.* was ending which left CBS with an expensive empty Hawaii studio?
8) What British comedy centers on the adventures of possibly the last human alive who is stranded 3 million years into the future on a mining ship?
9) What series was based on horror tales from EC Comics books of the 1950s?
10) The sitcom *The Hogan Family* was originally named after its star who left after two seasons while the series continued for three

more seasons; what was the original name?

Quiz 19 Answers

1) Vincent
2) Kevin Arnold
3) *The Kids in the Hall* (1988–1994)
4) *It's a Living* (1980–1989)
5) *Flamingo Road* (1980–1982)
6) *Perfect Strangers* (1986–1993)
7) *Jake and the Fatman* – The producers decided to have the Fatman move from Los Angeles to Hawaii and take his investigators with him. After the Hawaii studio lease expired, the series was returned to Los Angeles.
8) *Red Dwarf* – debuted in 1988
9) *Tales from the Crypt* (1989–1996)
10) *Valerie* (1986–1991) – Valerie Harper originally starred as the family's mother; when she left, Sandy Duncan was brought in as an aunt and mother figure.

1990s

Quiz 1

1) What was Ross' occupation on *Friends*?
2) In 1994, what show broke ground depicting a gay marriage between innkeepers Ron and Erick?
3) Who was the original host of Comedy Central's *The Daily Show*?
4) What is Judge Judy's last name?
5) What town was the setting for *Dr. Quinn, Medicine Woman*?
6) What character does Sean Hayes play on *Will & Grace*?
7) Beavis and Butt-Head wear shirts from what two rock bands on *Beavis and Butt-Head*?
8) What city was *Frasier* set in?
9) Who hosted the original primetime version of *Who Wants to Be a Millionaire*?
10) What was the name of Chris Noth's character who played Carrie's love interest on *Sex and the City*?

Quiz 1 Answers

1) Paleontologist
2) *Northern Exposure* (1990–1995)
3) Craig Kilborn
4) Sheindlin
5) Colorado Springs
6) Jack McFarland
7) AC/DC and Metallica
8) Seattle
9) Regis Philbin
10) Mr. Big

Quiz 2

1) Who played FBI Special Agent Dale Cooper on *Twin Peaks*?
2) Who played the title role on *Xena: Warrior Princess*?
3) On *Charmed*, what was the name of the book of witchcraft that was passed down to the sisters?
4) What was the family name of the aliens on *3rd Rock from the Sun*?

5) What crime comedy followed a cynical American police detective and an upright Royal Canadian Mounted Police constable in the city of Chicago?

6) Who was Conan O'Brien's sidekick on *Late Night with Conan O'Brien*?

7) What grade are the boys from *South Park* in?

8) What series centered on a minister, and his wife and their seven children?

9) Who starred as the young genius Quinn Mallory who creates a portal to parallel universes on *Sliders*?

10) What series featured Kermit the Frog again running a variety show?

Quiz 2 Answers

1) Kyle MacLachlan
2) Lucy Lawless
3) *Book of Shadows*
4) Solomon
5) *Due South* (1994–1999)
6) Andy Richter
7) 4th grade
8) *7th Heaven* (1996–2007)
9) Jerry O'Connell
10) *Muppets Tonight* (1996–1998)

Quiz 3

1) What sitcom was a continuation of *The Golden Girls* and starred three of the four original actresses?

2) What city was the setting for *The Drew Carey Show*?

3) Who played the talk show sidekick on *The Larry Sanders Show*?

4) What drama was based on five siblings who are left to find their own way after their parents are killed by a drunk driver?

5) What was the name of the airline run by the Hackett brothers on *Wings*?

6) On *The Fresh Prince of Bel-Air*, where was Will Smith's character from before moving to Bel-Air?

7) What was the name of Tim Taylor's television cohost on *Home Improvement*?

8) What was the first name of Walker on *Walker, Texas Ranger*?

9) What sitcom featured a recovering alcoholic who becomes the

manager of a big city bus station?

10) On *Frazier*, what was the name of the dad's dog?

Quiz 3 Answers

1) *The Golden Palace* (1992-1993)
2) Cleveland
3) Jeffrey Tambor
4) *Party of Five* (1990-2000)
5) Sandpiper Air
6) Philadelphia
7) Al Borland
8) Cordell
9) *The John Larroquette Show* (1993-1996)
10) Eddie

Quiz 4

1) Who was the only actor on *NYPD Blue* to stay with the series through its entire run and appear in every episode?
2) What sitcom featured three real life siblings playing siblings?
3) What game show featured Ben Stein as host and Jimmy Kimmel as co-host?
4) What host has been on the most *Dateline NBC* episodes?
5) What series that started in 1999 won the Drama Series Emmy each of its first four seasons?
6) Diedrich Bader's character on *The Drew Carey Show* is a jumbled version of a historical figure's name; what is it?
7) What action drama featured a clandestine anti-terrorist organization that fakes the death of a convicted murderer believing her beauty and killing ability will make her a valuable new operative?
8) Who played the captain on *Star Trek: Voyager*?
9) What sitcom featured a free-spirited yoga instructor and a conservative lawyer who get married on their first date?
10) Who played the title role on the sitcom *Boy Meets World*?

Quiz 4 Answers

1) Dennis Franz
2) *Everybody Loves Raymond* (1996-2005) - Real life siblings Madylin,

Sawyer and Sullivan Sweeten played the three children Ally, Geoffrey and Michael.

3) *Win Ben Stein's Money* (1997-2002)
4) Lester Holt
5) *The West Wing* (1999-2006)
6) Oswald Lee Harvey - after Lee Harvey Oswald
7) *La Femme Nikita* (1997-2001)
8) Kate Mulgrew
9) *Dharma & Greg* (1997-2002)
10) Ben Savage

Quiz 5

1) What was the name of Tony Shalhoub's character on *Wings*?
2) Who was the series creator and voiced the title characters on *Beavis and Butt-Head*?
3) What are the two main non-human races on *Babylon 5*?
4) What city was *ER* set in?
5) What series starred Brandy Norwood as a teenager living in the Leimert Park section of Los Angeles?
6) What state was *Twin Peaks* set in?
7) What was the name of Michael J. Fox's character on *Spin City*?
8) What sitcom had the character Ursula Buffay who was the twin of a character on a different sitcom?
9) Who played the title role on *Hercules: The Legendary Journeys*?
10) What series was about a pizza delivery boy who accidentally freezes himself and wakes up one thousand years in the future?

Quiz 5 Answers

1) Antonio Scarpacci
2) Mike Judge
3) Minbari and Centauri
4) Chicago
5) *Moesha* (1996-2001)
6) Washington
7) Mike Flaherty
8) *Mad About You* (1992-1999) - Ursula Buffay played by Lisa Kudrow was the twin sister of Phoebe Buffay also played by Lisa Kudrow on *Friends*.

9) Kevin Sorbo
10) *Futurama* (1999–2013)

Quiz 6

1) Who provided the voice for Turanga Leela on *Futurama*?
2) Who plays the title roles on *Will & Grace*?
3) What mystery crime drama starred a real-life father and son playing father and son?
4) What town was *Buffy the Vampire Slayer* set in?
5) On *The Fresh Prince of Bel-Air*, what was the full name of Will Smith's character?
6) What is Mariska Hargitay's character name on *Law & Order: Special Victims Unit*?
7) What animated series opening credits includes a spoof of the *All in the Family* opening with Edith playing the piano and singing with Archie?
8) What sitcom revolved around a fortysomething actress living in Los Angeles working in an industry that worships youth?
9) What animated series starred a psychotic Chihuahua and a dimwitted Manx cat in unusual adventures?
10) Who played Joey Potter on *Dawson's Creek*?

Quiz 6 Answers

1) Katey Sagal
2) Eric McCormack and Debra Messing
3) *Diagnosis Murder* (1993–2001) – starred Dick and Barry Van Dyke
4) Sunnydale
5) Will Smith – his own name
6) Olivia Benson
7) *Family Guy* –Lois plays the piano and sings with Peter.
8) *Cybill* (1995–1998)
9) *The Ren & Stimpy Show* (1991–1996)
10) Katie Holmes

Quiz 7

1) What were the names of the trio of angels on *Touched by an Angel*?
2) What action adventure show featured early 21st century submarine Captain Nathan Bridger keeping the peace and exploring the last

frontier on Earth?

3) On *The King of Queens*, what was Doug and Carrie's last name?

4) What is the name of the family on *Family Guy*?

5) What animated series was about the misadventures of a boy genius and his annoying sister?

6) What was the name of Richard Belzer's character on *Homicide: Life on the Street*?

7) What show was the longest running live action science fiction series until it was surpassed by *Supernatural* many years later?

8) What *Star Trek* series had the ship stranded 75,000 light years from home and facing an estimated 75-year trip home?

9) *Diagnosis Murder* was a spinoff of what show?

10) On *The King of Queens*, Doug was a delivery driver for what company?

Quiz 7 Answers

1) Monica, Tess, Andrew

2) *Seaquest DSV* (1993-1996)

3) Heffernan

4) Griffin

5) *Dexter's Laboratory* (1996-2003)

6) John Munch

7) *Stargate SG-1* (1997-2007)

8) *Star Trek: Voyager* (1995-2001)

9) *Jake and the Fatman*

10) International Parcel Service (IPS)

Quiz 8

1) What was Hank Hill's occupation on *King of the Hill*?

2) What famous author created *ER*?

3) Who played the title role on *Hangin' with Mr. Cooper*?

4) What children's animated series featured Lily Tomlin as Ms. Frizzle?

5) What animated science fiction comedy had character Tad Ghostal hosting his own late-night talk show filmed in outer space along with his cohost and former villain Zorak interviewing Earth celebrities through their video phone?

6) Who played station owner Jimmy James on *NewsRadio*?

7) What children's series is based on the books by Marc Brown and features the adventures of an 8-year-old aardvark and his family and friends?

8) What was the name of the underwater city where SpongeBob lives on *SpongeBob SquarePants*?

9) Who starred in the title role of Dr. Sam Waters on the crime drama *Profiler*?

10) In what state was the sitcom *That '70s Show* set?

Quiz 8 Answers

1) Propane salesman
2) Michael Crichton – author of *The Andromeda Strain, Jurassic Park, Rising Sun, Disclosure*
3) Mark Curry
4) *The Magic School Bus* (1994-1997)
5) *Space Ghost Coast to Coast* (1993-2008)
6) Stephen Root
7) *Arthur* – debuted in 1996
8) Bikini Bottom
9) Ally Walker
10) Wisconsin

Quiz 9

1) What was the first spinoff of *Beverly Hills, 90210*?
2) What comedy series had Jim Carrey, Jamie Foxx, and Jennifer Lopez?
3) What actor appeared in the most *ER* episodes?
4) Where was the crime drama *Silk Stockings* set?
5) In the sitcom *Ellen*, what was Ellen's occupation?
6) What was the name of the original DCI on the British detective drama *Midsomer Murders*?
7) What were the first names of the four lead female characters on *Sex and the City*?
8) What sitcom had Martin Lawrence playing a total of 10 characters over the series run?
9) What show frequently featured performers Wayne Brady, Ryan Stiles, and Colin Mochrie?
10) What sitcom featured a misanthropic doctor who runs a clinic in New York City?

Quiz 9 Answers

1) *Melrose Place* (1992–1999)
2) *In Living Color* (1990–1994)
3) Noah Wylie - 254 episodes
4) Palm Beach, Florida
5) Bookstore owner
6) Tom Barnaby
7) Carrie, Samantha, Charlotte, Miranda
8) *Martin* (1992–1997)
9) *Whose Line Is It Anyway?* (1998–2007)
10) *Becker* (1998–2004)

Quiz 10

1) Who played the alien leader The Big Giant Head on *3rd Rock from the Sun*?
2) What action series featured characters Reno Raines, Bobby Sixkiller, and Cheyenne Phillips working as bounty hunters?
3) What was the nanny's name on the sitcom *The Nanny*?
4) Who played Khadijah James on *Living Single*?
5) After 227 in 1985. what sitcom was the second ever to feature four African-American females as lead characters?
6) What was the precinct number on *NYPD Blue*?
7) What was the family name of the siblings on *Party of Five*?
8) Tom, Dick, and Harry were the names of the three main male characters on what sitcom?
9) What sitcom featured Frank Lambert, a construction worker, and Carol Foster, a beautician, who each have three children and have to learn to live together after spontaneously getting married?
10) On *The X-Files*, what was Mulder's nickname?

Quiz 10 Answers

1) William Shatner
2) *Renegade* (1992–1997) - starring Lorenzo Lamas
3) Fran Fine
4) Queen Latifah
5) *Living Single* (1993–1998)
6) 15th

7) Salinger
8) *3rd Rock from the Sun* (1996–2001)
9) *Step by Step* (1991–1998)
10) Spooky

Quiz 11

1) Who played Lois Lane on *Lois & Clark: The New Adventures of Superman?*
2) What children's animated series featured Tommy Pickles, Chuckie Finster, and Phil and Lil Deville as four babies?
3) Who played Maya Gallo on the sitcom *Just Shoot Me!*
4) Who played Don Johnson's partner on the police series *Nash Bridges?*
5) Who was *Law & Order: Special Victims Unit* actress Mariska Hargitay's mother?
6) Who played the psychotherapist Dr. Jennifer Melfi on *The Sopranos?*
7) On *Mad About You*, what was Paul Buchman's occupation?
8) What series centered on the lives of three young alien/human hybrids with extraordinary gifts?
9) What series featured clay figure announcers Johnny Gomez and Nick Diamond calling the action in sporting bouts?
10) Adrian Paul starred in what fantasy adventure series based on a movie of the same name?

Quiz 11 Answers

1) Teri Hatcher
2) *Rugrats* (1990–2006)
3) Laura San Giacomo
4) Cheech Marin
5) Jayne Mansfield
6) Lorraine Bracco
7) Filmmaker
8) *Roswell* (1999–2002)
9) *Celebrity Deathmatch* (1998–2007)
10) *Highlander* (1992–1998)

Quiz 12

1) What drama series had the tagline "Hero of a thousand faces. Man

of a thousand lives"?

2) What series won the Emmy for either Guest Actor in a Drama Series or Guest Actress in a Drama Series every year it was on from 1999 to 2004?

3) What series had 25 different actors fill the six regular roles on the show over its run?

4) What was the name of Xena's companion on her journeys on *Xena: Warrior Princess*?

5) Who played the title role on *Sabrina, the Teenage Witch*?

6) What show had the tagline "What if you had tomorrow's news... today?"

7) What series featured twins separated at birth who are reunited as teenagers?

8) What show was one of the first in the U.S. with a main character to come out as gay in real life and on the show in a 1997 episode?

9) What series had the theme song "Tossed Salad & Scrambled Eggs"?

10) What series featured Bruce Campbell as a Harvard educated bounty hunter in the Old West?

Quiz 12 Answers

1) *The Pretender* (1996-2000)
2) *The Practice*
3) *Law & Order* (1990-2010)
4) Gabrielle
5) Melissa Joan Hart
6) *Early Edition* (1996-2000)
7) *Sister, Sister* (1994-1999)
8) *Ellen* (1994-1998) - Ellen DeGeneres
9) Frasier (1993-2004)
10) *The Adventures of Brisco County, Jr.* (1993-1994)

Quiz 13

1) What normally indoor recreational item is outdoors in Drew's backyard on *The Drew Carey Show*?

2) Who played Dr. Joel Fleischman on *Northern Exposure*?

3) What was the spinoff of *Buffy the Vampire Slayer* called?

4) What show opens with "In the criminal justice system, sexually based offenses are considered especially heinous"?

5) What was the name of the department store where Drew works on

The Drew Carey Show?

6) What comedy was a look behind the scenes at a late-night talk show?
7) What sitcom featured Mr. Floppy, a boozing, chain-smoking stuffed gray rabbit voiced by Bobcat Goldthwait, whom the lead character consults for advice?
8) Who played the title role on *Dr. Quinn, Medicine Woman?*
9) On what island was the sitcom *Wings* set?
10) What are Will and Grace's occupations on *Will & Grace?*

Quiz 13 Answers

1) Pool table
2) Rob Morrow
3) *Angel* (1999-2004)
4) *Law & Order: Special Victims Unit* - debuted in 1999
5) Winfred-Louder
6) *The Larry Sanders Show* (1992-1998)
7) *Unhappily Ever After* (1995-1999)
8) Jane Seymour
9) Nantucket
10) Lawyer and interior designer

Quiz 14

1) What was the name of the coffee shop where the group hung out on *Friends?*
2) According to series creator Seth MacFarlane, what famous actor is the basis for Stewie's voice on *Family Guy?*
3) What was the name of the late-night sketch comedy show based on a magazine?
4) William B. Davis played a villain on *The X-Files* and didn't have a normal name; how was his character referred to?
5) Which *South Park* character has been killed dozens of times?
6) Who provided the voice for Jay Sherman, a New York film critic, who has to review films he doesn't like on the animated comedy *The Critic?*
7) What was the name of Mulder and Scully's supervisor on *The X-Files?*
8) What science fiction series featured astronaut John Crichton who is accidentally hurled across the universe into the midst of an

intergalactic conflict?

9) What was the name of Hercules' best friend who accompanied him on his journeys on *Hercules: The Legendary Journeys*?

10) Who is the creator of *Law & Order* and its spinoffs?

Quiz 14 Answers

1) Central Perk
2) Rex Harrison
3) *MADtv* (1995–2016)
4) Cigarette Smoking Man
5) Kenny
6) Jon Lovitz
7) Walter Skinner
8) *Farscape* (1999–2003)
9) Iolaus
10) Dick Wolf

Quiz 15

1) Who played the President on *The West Wing*?
2) What sitcom featured three twenty-somethings sharing a Boston apartment and hanging around and working at a pizza place?
3) Who played Lieutenant Colonel Sarah MacKenzie on *JAG*?
4) Who played the title role on the sitcom *Becker*?
5) In what state is *South Park* set?
6) Who played Bobby Donnell, the head of a struggling law firm, on *The Practice*?
7) What was the name of the Alaskan town *Northern Exposure* was set in?
8) In what century was *Babylon 5* set?
9) What was the name of the fashion magazine at the center of the sitcom *Just Shoot Me*!
10) What show featured Jason Priestley, Jennie Garth, Ian Ziering, Gabrielle Carteris, Brian Austin Green, and Tori Spelling?

Quiz 15 Answers

1) Martin Sheen
2) *Two Guys, a Girl and a Pizza Place* (1998–2001)
3) Catherine Bell

4) Ted Danson
5) Colorado
6) Dylan McDermott
7) Cicely
8) 23rd century
9) *Blush*
10) *Beverly Hills, 90210* (1990–2000)

Quiz 16

1) Who played the title role on *Angel?*
2) What animated show featured the adventures of a cowardly dog who must defend his unknowing farmer owners from all kinds of dangers?
3) What was the name of Dennis Franz's character on *NYPD Blue?*
4) What was the name of the snobbish housewife determined to climb the social ladder on the British comedy *Keeping Up Appearances?*
5) What sitcom starred Lea Thompson as a successful cartoonist living in Manhattan?
6) What was the first *Law & Order* spinoff?
7) Who played the mayor on the sitcom *Spin City?*
8) In *Early Edition*, what was the name of the paper from the future that Gary receives?
9) On *Buffy the Vampire Slayer*, what was Buffy's last name?
10) What medical drama featured Adam Arkin, Hector Elizondo, Mark Harmon, and Mandy Patinkin?

Quiz 16 Answers

1) David Boreanaz
2) *Courage the Cowardly Dog* (1999–2002)
3) Andy Sipowicz
4) Hyacinth Bucket
5) *Caroline in the City* (1995–1999)
6) *Law & Order: Special Victims Unit* (1999)
7) Barry Bostwick
8) Chicago Sun Times
9) Summers
10) Chicago Hope (1994–2000)

Quiz 17

1) Who played Arthur Spooner on *The King of Queens?*
2) What sitcom featured a divorced female recovering alcoholic struggling to bring up three children on her own?
3) What was the name of the family that *Picket Fences* centered on?
4) What sitcom featured prehistoric Jim Henson animatronic characters?
5) What was the last name of the three sisters who were witches on *Charmed?*
6) What was George Clooney's character name on *ER?*
7) What series starred Keri Russell as a girl fresh out of high school who followed her high school crush to college to be near him?
8) What sitcom featured the pick-up line, "How you doin?"
9) What character on *Family Guy* is voiced by the show's creator Seth MacFarlane in his natural speaking voice?
10) *Xena: Warrior Princess* was a spinoff of what show?

Quiz 17 Answers

1) Jerry Stiller
2) *Grace Under Fire* (1993-1998)
3) Brock
4) *Dinosaurs* (1991-1994)
5) Halliwell
6) Doug Ross
7) *Felicity* (1998-2002)
8) *Friends* (1994-2004) – Joey's line
9) Brian – the dog
10) *Hercules: The Legendary Journeys* (1995-1999)

Quiz 18

1) What animated series had a genius who was modeled after Orson Welles and his sidekick trying to conquer the world each night?
2) What was the first name of Dr. Niles Crane's wife who was frequently talked about but never seen on *Frasier?*
3) Who played the title role on *The Nanny?*
4) What was the first name only that the title character of *The Pretender* was known as?
5) Who was the creator and voice of the starring character on the

animated sitcom *King of the Hill?*

6) Who created *The West Wing* and wrote many of its episodes?

7) What sitcom ran the most first run episodes in the 1990s?

8) What was the brand name of the tools that Tim promoted on his television show on *Home Improvement?*

9) What British sitcom was about two best friends, Edina Monsoon and Patsy Stone, who are constantly drugged up and outrageously selfish?

10) On the prison drama *Oz,* what was the name of the experimental unit of the prison?

Quiz 18 Answers

1) *Pinky and the Brain* (1995–1998)

2) Maris

3) Fran Drescher

4) Jarrod

5) Mike Judge

6) Aaron Sorkin

7) *The Simpsons*

8) Binford Tools

9) *Absolutely Fabulous* (1992–2012)

10) Emerald City

Quiz 19

1) The main characters on *Friends* are all named after characters from what television show?

2) What teen sitcom starred James Franco, Seth Rogan, and Jason Segel?

3) What was the name of Sabrina's talking cat on *Sabrina, the Teenage Witch?*

4) What do the initials stand for in the series title *JAG?*

5) What are the first names of the four main boys on *South Park?*

6) What was the name of the small town plagued by bizarre and violent crimes on *Picket Fences?*

7) Jon Lovitz replaced Phil Hartman on his death in what sitcom?

8) What was the name of the space station leader on *Star Trek: Deep Space Nine?*

9) Who played Jamie Buchman on the sitcom *Mad About You?*

10) What was the family name on *Everybody Loves Raymond*?

Quiz 19 Answers

1) *All My Children*
2) *Freaks and Geeks* (1999–2000)
3) Salem
4) Judge Advocate General
5) Stan, Kyle, Eric, Kenny
6) Rome, Wisconsin
7) *NewsRadio* (1995–1999)
8) Benjamin Sisko
9) Helen Hunt
10) Barone

Quiz 20

1) All but one of the five main cast members on *Everybody Loves Raymond* won Emmys for their performances; which actor was nominated but never won an Emmy?
2) What drama focused on three generations of women living together in Hartford, Connecticut with one of them working as a family court judge?
3) What always arrived along with the future newspaper on *Early Edition*?
4) What animated children's series featured siblings Wakko, Yakko, and Dot?
5) Who played the title role on *Ally McBeal*?
6) Who played the school principal on the sitcom *Boy Meets World*?
7) What classic science fiction anthology series was revived in the 1990s and had a longer run than the original?
8) What was the name of Fox Mulder's partner on *The X-Files*?
9) Who played the title role on the sitcom *Blossom*?
10) Who took over the role Kurt Russell played in the movie *Stargate* on the series *Stargate SG-1*?

Quiz 20 Answers

1) Peter Boyle
2) *Judging Amy* (1999–2006)
3) Cat

4) *Animaniacs* (1993–1998)
5) Calista Flockhart
6) William Daniels
7) *The Outer Limits* (1995–2002)
8) Dana Scully
9) Mayim Bialik
10) Richard Dean Anderson

2000s

Quiz 1

1) What is the name of the FBI unit the team works for on *Criminal Minds*?
2) Who played the title role on the medical drama *House*?
3) What was the name of the central family on the sitcom *The Middle*?
4) Who played Ed Deline, the head of the casino surveillance team, on the drama *Las Vegas*?
5) What series featured an FBI agent working with a formerly institutionalized scientist and his son to investigate unexplained phenomena?
6) What is the name of the sarcastic space alien on the animated sitcom *American Dad*?
7) Besides Penny, who is the only main character on *The Big Bang Theory* who doesn't have a PhD?
8) What was the name of the serial killer that *The Mentalist* was after for the murder of his wife and daughter?
9) What series has the tagline "To catch a criminal, you have to think like one"?
10) What is the name of the dad and CIA agent on the animated sitcom *American Dad*?

Quiz 1 Answers

1) Behavioral Analysis Unit (BAU)
2) Hugh Laurie
3) Heck
4) James Caan
5) *Fringe* (2008-2013)
6) Roger
7) Howard Wolowitz – He has a master's degree in aerospace engineering.
8) Red John
9) *Criminal Minds* – debuted in 2005
10) Stan Smith

Quiz 2

1) *Glee* was set at what high school?
2) On the sitcom *Parks and Recreation*, what instrument did Ron Swanson secretly play professionally?
3) What was Kyra Sedgwick's character name on the police drama *The Closer*?
4) What series centered on Clark Kent as a teen in Kansas?
5) Where was the crime drama *Veronica Mars* set?
6) What city was the setting for the crime drama *Dexter*?
7) What crime drama focused on Baltimore's inner-city drug scene?
8) *Torchwood* was a spinoff of what series?
9) Who played the ethically challenged attorney Alan Shore on the crime drama *Boston Legal*?
10) Who played Nathan Ford, the leader of a group of high-tech crooks who help people, on *Leverage*?

Quiz 2 Answers

1) William McKinley
2) Saxophone
3) Brenda Johnson
4) *Smallville* (2001–2011)
5) Neptune, California
6) Miami
7) *The Wire* (2002–2008)
8) *Doctor Who*
9) James Spader
10) Timothy Hutton

Quiz 3

1) What was the name of the electronics store Chuck continued to work at as a cover while he was a spy on *Chuck*?
2) What is the name of the hospital in *Grey's Anatomy*?
3) Who played the title role on the series *Nurse Jackie*?
4) What was the name of the chicken restaurant chain owned by Gustavo on *Breaking Bad*?
5) What is the name of Mark Harmon's character on *NCIS*?
6) What are the first names of the brother and sister central

characters on *It's Always Sunny in Philadelphia*?

7) What character did Bryan Cranston play on *Breaking Bad*?

8) What sitcom starred Courteney Cox and featured the relationships of a group of neighbors living in Gulfhaven, Florida?

9) What was the name of the computerized information that Chuck accidentally downloaded into his brain making him a valuable spy asset on *Chuck*?

10) What is the name of the central family on *Arrested Development*?

Quiz 3 Answers

1) Buy More
2) Seattle Grace
3) Edie Falco
4) Los Pollos Hermanos
5) Leroy Jethro Gibbs
6) Dennis and Dee Reynolds
7) Walter White
8) *Cougar Town* (2009–2015)
9) Intersect
10) Bluth

Quiz 4

1) Who played the role of Dr. Jordan Cavanaugh, a Boston forensic pathologist, on *Crossing Jordan*?

2) In the sitcom *Community*, the original study group was formed for what subject?

3) Who played head detective Mac Taylor on *CSI: NY*?

4) Who played the title role on the crime comedy *Monk*?

5) Will Schuester, the glee club director on *Glee*, teaches what subject?

6) On *Heroes*, common people realize they have superpowers, and Zachary Quinto played a serial killer out to gain their powers by killing them; what was his character name?

7) What state was the sitcom *Community* set in?

8) Who played the title role on the sitcom *According to Jim*?

9) Who played the title role on the sitcom *Malcolm in the Middle*?

10) What series was set in the late 1800s in a deeply corrupt and crime ridden town?

Quiz 4 Answers

1) Jill Hennessy
2) Spanish
3) Gary Sinise
4) Tony Shalhoub
5) Spanish
6) Skylar
7) Colorado
8) Jim Belushi
9) Frankie Muniz
10) *Deadwood* (2004-2006)

Quiz 5

1) Who starred as firefighter Tommy Gavin who deals with the fears of his job and his personal problems in the comedy drama *Rescue Me*?
2) In *The Good Wife*, the title character's husband is imprisoned for a sex and corruption scandal; what was the husband's occupation?
3) Who starred in the title role on the teen series *Hannah Montana*?
4) What city was the crime comedy *Psych* set in?
5) Who played the title role on the sitcom *Ugly Betty*?
6) Who was the only actor to appear on the 1970s *Battlestar Galactica* and the revived 2000s series?
7) Tim Roth starred as Dr. Cal Lightman, the world's leading deception expert who studies facial expressions and involuntary body language, in what series?
8) What comedy drama featured a young ER doctor who was wrongly blamed for a patient's death and moved to the Hamptons and became a concierge doctor to the rich and famous?
9) What drama series was about the reign and marriages of King Henry VIII?
10) What science fiction series featured former galactic war veteran Malcolm Reynolds as captain of the transport ship *Serenity*?

Quiz 5 Answers

1) Dennis Leary
2) State attorney
3) Miley Cyrus

4) Santa Barbara, California
5) America Ferrera
6) Richard Hatch
7) *Lie to Me* (2009–2011)
8) *Royal Pains* (2009–2016)
9) *The Tudors* (2007–2010)
10) *Firefly* (2002–2003)

Quiz 6

1) What series featured a mild-mannered police analyst who was also a serial killer?
2) In what city was *Breaking Bad* primarily set?
3) In the science fiction series *Warehouse 13*, where was the warehouse located?
4) What series featured a pie-maker who can bring dead people back to life and solves murder mysteries?
5) What city was the U.S. sitcom *The Office* set in?
6) *Burn Notice* was about a discredited spy who helps people in need; where was it set?
7) What was the name of the glee club on *Glee*?
8) What sports drama series was based on a 2004 movie of the same name?
9) What teen drama was a reboot of a 1990s series with a Kansas family relocating to Beverly Hills?
10) Who plays Dr. Meredith Grey on *Grey's Anatomy*?

Quiz 6 Answers

1) *Dexter* (2006–2013)
2) Albuquerque, New Mexico
3) South Dakota
4) *Pushing Daisies* (2007–2009)
5) Scranton, Pennsylvania
6) Miami
7) New Directions
8) *Friday Night Lights* (2006–2011)
9) *90210* (2008–2013)
10) Ellen Pompeo

Quiz 7

1) What was the original name of the advertising firm at the center of *Mad Men*?
2) What series showed the aftermath of a nearby nuclear explosion on a small peaceful town?
3) Who played the original head of the *CSI: Crime Scene Investigation* unit?
4) What sitcom starred Thomas Jane as a struggling suburban Detroit high school coach who resorts to male prostitution?
5) What was the first name of the character played by Ashton Kutcher on *Two and a Half Men*?
6) What series was set in cozy little Northwestern town where the best minds in the U.S. have secretly been placed to build futuristic inventions?
7) What British comedy drama centers on a socially challenged doctor who moves from London to Cornwall?
8) *NCIS* is a spinoff of what series?
9) Who played the title role on the action adventure comedy *Chuck*?
10) What was the *Stargate* spinoff that was set in the Pegasus Galaxy and featured a new enemy, The Wraith?

Quiz 7 Answers

1) Sterling Cooper
2) *Jericho* (2006-2008)
3) William Peterson
4) *Hung* (2009-2011)
5) Walden
6) *Eureka* (2006-2012)
7) *Doc Martin* – debuted 2004
8) *JAG*
9) Zachary Levi
10) *Stargate: Atlantis* (2004-2009)

Quiz 8

1) Who starred as housewife and mother Allison DuBois who uses her psychic visions to work as a part-time consultant for the district attorney's office on *Medium*?
2) In what century was *Star Trek: Enterprise* set?

3) *Boston Legal* was a spinoff of what series?

4) Jeffrey Donovan played the discredited spy on *Burn Notice*; what was his character name?

5) Who played the role of Sydney Bristow on the action drama *Alias*?

6) What was the name of the town that was the setting for *Parks and Recreation*?

7) What series centered on the members of a dysfunctional California family that runs an independent funeral home?

8) What was the first name of the dad played by Bryan Cranston on the sitcom *Malcolm in the Middle*?

9) What was the captain's name on *Star Trek: Enterprise*?

10) What actor took over as the second leader of the *CSI: Crime Scene Investigation* unit?

Quiz 8 Answers

1) Patricia Arquette
2) 22nd century – from 2151 to 2155
3) *The Practice*
4) Michael Westen
5) Jennifer Garner
6) Pawnee, Indiana
7) *Six Feet Under* (2001–2005)
8) Hal
9) Jonathan Archer
10) Laurence Fishburne

Quiz 9

1) On *CSI: Miami*, who played Horatio Caine, the leader of the unit?

2) What sitcom starred Patrick Warburton, Megyn Price, Oliver Hudson, Bianca Kajlich, and David Spade?

3) What series centered on cases of an FBI unit specializing in missing person investigations and starred Anthony LaPaglia and Poppy Montgomery?

4) On *Criminal Minds*, what term do they typically use to refer to an unknown perpetrator of a crime?

5) What was the name of the hospital on *House*?

6) What was the name of Jane Lynch's cheer leading coach character on *Glee*?

7) On *Monk*, what condition did Monk suffer from?

8) What crime series is set in the 1890s and very early 1900s and features a police detective solving crimes using scientific methods like fingerprints and lie detecting machines way ahead of their time?

9) Who played the commander of *Battlestar Galactica* in the reboot series?

10) What crime comedy featured the lives of incompetent Nevada sheriff's deputies in a mockumentary style parody?

Quiz 9 Answers

1) David Caruso
2) *Rules of Engagement* (2007–2013)
3) *Without a Trace* (2002–2009)
4) Unsub – for unknown subject
5) Princeton–Plainsboro Teaching Hospital (PPTH) – New Jersey
6) Sue Sylvester
7) Obsessive-compulsive disorder (OCD)
8) *Murdoch Mysteries* – debuted 2008
9) Edward James Olmos
10) *Reno 911!* (2003–2009)

Quiz 10

1) Who played Dr. Jack Shephard on *Lost*?
2) Who plays the role of Phil Dunphy on *Modern Family*?
3) On *Castle*, what was the name of the fictional heroine Castle created for his books based on working with Kate?
4) What series featured half-brothers Lucas and Nathan Scott on and off the basketball court in a small North Carolina town?
5) What was Marshall's occupation on the sitcom *How I Met Your Mother*?
6) What role did Dennis Haysbert play on the drama *24*?
7) Who is the only main actor on *The Big Bang Theory* who has a PhD in real life?
8) Who played Barney on *How I Met Your Mother*?
9) Who was the creator of the science fiction adventure *Firefly*?
10) Neil Flynn, who played the dad on *The Middle*, also played a janitor on *Scrubs*; what was his character name on *Scrubs*?

Quiz 10 Answers

1) Matthew Fox
2) Ty Burrell
3) Nikki Heat
4) *One Tree Hill* (2003–2012)
5) Lawyer
6) President David Palmer
7) Mayim Bialik has a PhD in neuroscience.
8) Neil Patrick Harris
9) Joss Whedon
10) Janitor – He wasn't given a name.

Quiz 11

1) What British science fiction series featured Captain Jack Harkness who was a member of a renegade criminal investigation group founded by Queen Victoria to battle hostile extraterrestrial and supernatural threats?
2) What sitcom starred Danny McBride as a burned-out MLB pitcher who goes home to North Carolina to work as a gym teacher at his old middle school?
3) What was the name of the institute that Dr. Brennan works for on *Bones*?
4) The entire series *How I Met Your Mother* was told from the perspective of what character?
5) What state was the sitcom *The Middle* set in?
6) Sheldon on *The Big Bang Theory* is from what state?
7) On the science fiction mystery *Fringe*, what was the name of the huge global company that was frequently at the center of the investigations?
8) What was the name of the government law enforcement agency *The Mentalist* worked for?
9) Who played the title role on *Bones*?
10) Who played the boss on the original British mockumentary series *The Office*?

Quiz 11 Answers

1) *Torchwood* (2006–2011)
2) *Eastbound & Down* (2009–2013)

3) Jeffersonian
4) Ted Mosby
5) Indiana
6) Texas
7) Massive Dynamic
8) California Bureau of Investigation (CBI)
9) Emily Deschanel
10) Ricky Gervais

Quiz 12

1) What series centered on a young college graduate who was recruited her freshman year as a secret CIA agent and years later learned that she was actually part of a rogue international agency out to rule the world?
2) What is the family name of the two brothers on *Supernatural*?
3) Who played the role of Olive Snook on the comedy fantasy *Pushing Daisies*?
4) What action drama stared Jessica Alba as Max Guevera, a genetically enhanced superhuman prototype, searching for others like her and battling corruption in a post-apocalyptic Pacific Northwest?
5) What was Earl's last name on the sitcom *My Name is Earl*?
6) What drama centered on a biker who struggles to balance being a father and being involved in an outlaw motorcycle club?
7) What science fiction series about an extraterrestrial race arriving on Earth was a reboot of a 1980s miniseries and series?
8) What series featured a troubled youth who gets involved in the lives of a group of people in the wealthy area of Newport Beach, California?
9) What was Matt LeBlanc's spinoff from *Friends*?
10) On *Dexter*, the title character was a police analyst; what was his specialty?

Quiz 12 Answers

1) *Alias* (2001–2006)
2) Winchester
3) Kristin Chenoweth
4) *Dark Angel* (2000–2002)
5) Hickey

6) *Sons of Anarchy* (2008–2014)
7) *V* (2009–2011)
8) *The O.C.* (2003–2007)
9) *Joey* (2004–2006)
10) Blood splatter

Quiz 13

1) What crime drama is set in Los Angeles and features agents G. Callen and Sam Hanna?
2) Who played the agent Ari Gold on the sitcom *Entourage*?
3) What was Rainn Wilson's character name on *The Office*?
4) Who played the title role on the sitcom *My Name is Earl*?
5) Who played the captain on *Star Trek: Enterprise*?
6) *Private Practice* was a spinoff of what show?
7) What dos the title *NCIS* stand for?
8) What was Charlie Harper's occupation on the sitcom *Two and a Half Men*?
9) What is the first name of the forensic scientist played by Pauley Perrette on *NCIS*?
10) The crime drama *Murdoch Mysteries* is set in what Canadian city?

Quiz 13 Answers

1) NCIS: Los Angeles – debuted in 2009
2) Jeremy Piven
3) Dwight Schrute
4) Jason Lee
5) Scott Bakula
6) *Grey's Anatomy*
7) Naval Criminal Investigative Service
8) Jingle writer
9) Abby – Perrette has a college degree in forensics.
10) Toronto

Quiz 14

1) What was the name of Zach Braff's character on *Scrubs*?
2) What series had Teri Hatcher, Felicity Huffman, Eva Longoria, and Marcia Cross in the starring roles?
3) What animated sitcom features the employees of an international

spy agency?

4) What science fiction series featured two U.S Secret Service agents who must retrieve supernatural objects called artifacts?

5) The sitcom *Reba* which starred Reba McEntire was set in what city?

6) What stop motion animation series features voice work by Seth Green who is also one of the creators?

7) Who played the Sherlock Holmes like detective Robert Goran on *Law & Order: Criminal Intent*?

8) On *Private Practice*, what was the specialty of lead character Dr. Addison Forbes Montgomery played by Kate Walsh?

9) What was the name of the airline of the crashed plane on *Lost*?

10) What was the name of Chris Pratt's character on the sitcom *Parks and Recreation*?

Quiz 14 Answers

1) Dr. John "J.D." Dorian
2) *Desperate Housewives* (2004-2012)
3) *Archer* – debuted 2009
4) *Warehouse 13* (2009-2014)
5) Houston, Texas
6) *Robot Chicken* – debuted in 2005
7) Vincent D'Onofrio
8) Neonatal surgeon
9) Oceanic
10) Andy Dwyer

Quiz 15

1) What was the name of the state penitentiary in *Prison Break*?

2) The characters played by Jim Parsons and Johnny Galecki on *The Big Bang Theory* are named after who?

3) What is the name of the German speaking goldfish who was a result of a CIA experiment gone wrong on the animated sitcom *American Dad*?

4) Who played the title role on the drama *The Good Wife*?

5) What series was set in Louisiana and had humans and vampires coexisting?

6) What was the name of the legal firm on *Boston Legal*?

7) What comedy drama featured Hank Moody, a self-loathing, narcissistic author, drug user, alcoholic, and borderline sex addict?

8) What sitcom centered on a low-life who realized that his bad luck was a result of karma and sets out to make amends to all the people he had hurt?
9) What was the name of the hospital on the sitcom *Scrubs*?
10) What was the name of Tina Fey's character on *30 Rock*?

Quiz 15 Answers

1) Fox River
2) Sheldon Leonard – famous television producer and actor
3) Klaus
4) Julianna Margulies
5) *True Blood* (2008–2014)
6) Crane, Poole, and Schmidt
7) *Californication* (2007–2014)
8) *My Name is Earl* (2005–2009)
9) Sacred Heart
10) Liz Lemon

Quiz 16

1) What was the first ABC series in 22 years since *The Wonder Years* in 1988 to win the Outstanding Comedy Series Emmy?
2) What role does *Seinfeld* co-creator Larry David play on *Curb Your Enthusiasm*?
3) What was the name of Kiefer Sutherland's character on the drama *24*?
4) What was the third series in the *Law & Order* franchise?
5) What series had charming con artist Neal Caffrey helping the FBI catch elusive criminals in exchange for his freedom?
6) What series followed a dirty Los Angeles cop and the unit under his command?
7) What sitcom originally starred John Ritter, Katey Sagal, and Kaley Cuoco?
8) On what action drama series were all actors and actresses required to have their hair trimmed every five days?
9) Who plays the brother Dean on *Supernatural*?
10) On the sitcom *Entourage*, what was the name of the film star who was at the center of the series?

Quiz 16 Answers

1) *Modern Family* – debuted 2009
2) Larry David - He plays himself.
3) Jack Bauer
4) *Law & Order: Criminal Intent* (2001–2011)
5) *White Collar* (2009–2014)
6) *The Shield* (2002–2008)
7) *8 Simple Rules* (2002–2005) - John Ritter died after the first season, and the show continued without him.
8) 24 - Each season represents one day.
9) Jensen Ackles
10) Vince Chase

Quiz 17

1) On the crime comedy *Monk*, what was Monk's first name?
2) What sitcom was based on Fernando Gaitán's Colombian telenovela *Yo soy Betty, la fea* which had many other international adaptations?
3) What sitcom followed a group of old friends in a fantasy football league?
4) Who starred in the title role on *Veronica Mars*?
5) Who played Sam Axe, the former Navy Seal and best friend of the lead character, on *Burn Notice*?
6) What was the name of the title character on *The Mentalist*?
7) What crime series featured a female Philadelphia police detective working in the homicide department who is assigned crimes that were committed many years before and have not been solved?
8) Who played Detective Kate Beckett on the crime dramedy *Castle*?
9) Who played the brilliant, ruthless lawyer Patty Hewes on the legal thriller series *Damages*?
10) Who played Frankie, the mother, on the sitcom *The Middle*?

Quiz 17 Answers

1) Adrian
2) *Ugly Betty* (2006–2010)
3) *The League* (2009–2015)
4) Kristen Bell
5) Bruce Campbell

6) Patrick Jane
7) *Cold Case* (2003–2010)
8) Stana Katic
9) Glenn Close
10) Patricia Heaton

Quiz 18

1) What romance drama centered on privileged teens living on the Upper East Side of New York City?
2) On the U.S. series *The Office*, what was the name of the company they work for?
3) Who plays the role of Lucille Austero on *Arrested Development*?
4) What was the name of the sketch comedy show they were creating within the sitcom *30 Rock*?
5) What crime series featured U.S. Marshal Mary Shannon who spends her time relocating federal witnesses?
6) What was the name of the community college on *Community*?
7) What is the name of the Irish pub that is central to *It's Always Sunny in Philadelphia*?
8) What comedy drama centered on a suburban mother who starts dealing marijuana to maintain her lifestyle after her husband dies?
9) What supernatural series had brothers Stefan and Damon Salvatore returning to their home of Mystic Falls, Virginia?
10) What sitcom was based on the childhood experiences of comedian Chris Rock?

Quiz 18 Answers

1) *Gossip Girl* (2007–2012)
2) Dunder Mifflin Paper Company
3) Liza Minnelli
4) *TGS* – It was originally titled *The Girlie Show* before they brought in Tracy Jordan.
5) *In Plain Sight* (2008–2012)
6) Greendale
7) Paddy's
8) *Weeds* (2005–2012)
9) *The Vampire Diaries* (2009–2017)
10) *Everybody Hates Chris* (2005–2009)

Quiz 19

1) What drama focused on the business and personal lives of two plastic surgeons?
2) What was the name of the fictional casino which was the setting for the drama *Las Vegas*?
3) What was the name of the fashion magazine where Betty worked on *Ugly Betty*?
4) What character did James Roday play on *Psych*?
5) What was the name of Jon Hamm's character on *Mad Men*?
6) Where did the title for the sitcom *30 Rock* come from?
7) On *Bones*, what was the real first name of the title character?
8) Who played the sheriff on *Eureka*?
9) Who starred as Captain Dylan Hunt who is frozen in time for 300 years and along with his sentient warship *Andromeda* sets out to restore peace to the universe on the science fiction series *Andromeda*?
10) What sitcom starred Ricky Gervais as an actor reduced to working as an extra whose attempts to boost his career end in failure and embarrassment?

Quiz 19 Answers

1) *Nip/Tuck* (2003–2010)
2) Montecito
3) *Mode*
4) Shawn Spencer
5) Don Draper
6) 30 Rockefeller Plaza – It is the address for the NBC studios where *Saturday Night Live* is produced; series creator Tina Fey was a head writer and performer for *SNL* and based the show on her experiences there.
7) Temperance
8) Colin Ferguson
9) Kevin Sorbo
10) *Extras* (2005–2007)

Quiz 20

1) What is the name of the electronic musical instrument controlled without physical contact that Sheldon sometimes plays on *The Big*

Bang Theory?

2) What dramedy centers on the relationship between a thirtysomething single mother and her teen daughter living in Stars Hollow, Connecticut?

3) Who provides the narration on the sitcom *Arrested Development*?

4) The character Charlie Pace on *Lost* was a member of a one hit band; what was the band's name?

5) The actors who played what two characters on *The Office* went to high school together in real life?

6) What comedy drama starred a vapid model killed in a car crash who is brought back to life as an intelligent overweight lawyer?

7) On *Dexter*, what was the name of Dexter's boat that he frequently used to dispose of bodies?

8) The title for *Grey's Anatomy* is a reference to what book?

9) What science fiction drama dealt with decades of missing persons returned by a ball of light without any signs of aging and with many of them having heightened abilities?

10) What crime drama had a mathematician helping his FBI brother solve crimes?

Quiz 20 Answers

1) Theremin – Jim Parsons is really playing it on the show; the instrument was invented by Russian Leon Theremin in 1928.

2) *Gilmore Girls* (2000–2007)

3) Ron Howard – He wasn't intended to be permanent; he filled in the role on the pilot, and it worked out.

4) Drive Shaft

5) Jim Halpert and Ryan Howard – John Krasinski and B.J. Novak both went to Newton South High School in Newton, Massachusetts, and both graduated in 1997. They were even on the same little league baseball team.

6) *Drop Dead Diva* (2009–2014)

7) *Slice of Life*

8) *Gray's Anatomy of the Human Body* – written by Henry Gray

9) *The 4400* (2004–2007)

10) *Numb3rs* (2005–2010)

2010s

Quiz 1

1) What crime drama featured U.S. Marshal Raylan Givens who was reassigned from Miami to his childhood home in the rural Kentucky and was based on the character created by novelist Elmore Leonard?

2) The crime drama *The Killing* had Det. Sarah Linden investigating the death of Rosie Larsen who was found in the trunk of a car at the bottom of a lake; what city was the series set in?

3) On *Hawaii 5-0*, why does Steve McGarrett come to Hawaii?

4) What were the names of the three male characters Jess lived with on the sitcom *New Girl*?

5) On the superhero drama *Agents of S.H.I.E.L.D.*, what does S.H.I.E.L.D. stand for?

6) Who plays Detective Jake Peralta on the crime comedy *Brooklyn Nine-Nine*?

7) Who plays Dwayne Pride, leader of the NCIS team, on *NCIS: New Orleans*?

8) What spinoff sitcom has a leading character played by the real-life daughter of the actress who played the same role in the original series?

9) What actor on the sitcom *Superstore* is a former cast member of *The Kids in the Hall* and *Saturday Night Live*?

10) What science fiction series set in Chester's Mill, Maine was based on a Stephen King novel?

Quiz 1 Answers

1) *Justified* (2010-2015)
2) Seattle
3) Avenge his father's death
4) Nick, Schmidt, Winston
5) Strategic Homeland Intervention, Enforcement and Logistics Division
6) Andy Samberg
7) Scott Bakula
8) *Young Sheldon* - Zoe Perry who plays Sheldon's mother is the real-life daughter of Laurie Metcalf who plays Sheldon's mother on *The

Big Bang Theory.

9) Mark McKinney - He plays the store manager Glenn and was one of *The Kids in the Hall* and a *SNL* cast member from 1995 to 1997.

10) *Under the Dome* (2013-2015)

Quiz 2

1) What comedy followed the life of a divorced comedian living in New York with two kids?

2) What sitcom starred Adam Devine, Blake Anderson, and Anders Holm as friends who worked together as telemarketers?

3) What is Lucifer's last name on the fantasy drama *Lucifer*?

4) For what series did Rachel Brosnahan win the 2018 Outstanding Lead Actress in a Comedy Series Emmy?

5) *American Housewife* centers on mother Katie raising her flawed family in a wealthy town filled with perfect wives and their perfect offspring; what town is it set in?

6) What sitcom centered on a young OB/GYN doctor trying to balance her personal and professional life?

7) What actress won six consecutive Outstanding Lead Actress in a Comedy Series Emmys from 2012-2017?

8) What crime drama set in Los Angeles features a fixer for the rich and famous who makes their problems go away?

9) What was the name of the all-knowing, all seeing artificial intelligence created by Harold Finch on *Person of Interest*?

10) What science fiction drama had a young woman witnessing a suicide and assuming the look alike woman's identity and discovering that she and the dead woman are clones?

Quiz 2 Answers

1) *Louie* (2010-2015)

2) *Workaholics* (2011-2017)

3) Morningstar

4) *The Marvelous Mrs. Maisel* - debuted 2017

5) Westport, Connecticut

6) *The Mindy Project* (2012-2017)

7) Julia Louis-Dreyfus - *Veep*

8) *Ray Donovan* - debuted 2013

9) The Machine

10) *Orphan Black* (2013-2017)

Quiz 3

1) Who played the eventual U.S. President Claire Underwood on *House of Cards*?
2) What anthology crime drama was Jessica Biel's first leading role in a television series?
3) What teen mystery thriller was loosely based on the series of novels of the same name written by Sara Shepard?
4) On *Game of Thrones*, what is the name of the brotherhood that defends the realm against the creatures north of the wall?
5) What was the first show in producer Dick Wolf's set of four Chicago based series released in the 2010s?
6) What were the first names of the title characters in *2 Broke Girls*?
7) What fantasy drama series featured the lead character Scott McCall and was based on a 1985 movie of the same name?
8) What is the name of the evil multi-national corporation that the hackers target on *Mr. Robot*?
9) What sitcom is a spinoff of *The Goldbergs* and is set in the 1990s at William Penn Academy?
10) Who plays the title role on the crime drama *The Rookie*?

Quiz 3 Answers

1) Robin Wright
2) *The Sinner* – debuted 2017
3) *Pretty Little Liars* (2010-2017)
4) Night's Watch
5) *Chicago Fire* – It debuted in 2012 and was followed by *Chicago P.D.*, *Chicago Med*, and *Chicago Justice*.
6) Max and Caroline
7) Teen Wolf (2011-2017)
8) E-Corp
9) *Schooled* – debuted 2019
10) Nathan Fillion

Quiz 4

1) Thandie Newton won a 2018 Outstanding Supporting Actress in a Drama Series Emmy for what series?
2) Who plays Sherlock Holmes on *Elementary*?
3) *Game of Thrones* is based on a series of novels by what author?

4) What crime documentary was filmed over 10 years and tells the story of Steven Avery who served 18 years in prison for a wrongful conviction of sexual assault and attempted murder and then was charged with murder two years after he was released?

5) *Better Call Saul* is a spinoff of what series?

6) Who plays the title role of June Osborne in *The Handmaid's Tale*?

7) On *Sherlock*, Dr. Watson who is played by Morgan Freeman is a veteran of what war?

8) What sitcom shows the lives of three generations of the Short family told in four short stories?

9) What is the first primetime U.S. series starring an Asian-American family since Margaret Cho's *All-American Girl* in 1994?

10) What series was a spinoff from *The Vampire Diaries* and centered on the Mikaelson siblings, the world's first vampires?

Quiz 4 Answers

1) *Westworld* – debuted 2016
2) Jonny Lee Miller
3) George R.R. Martin
4) *Making a Murderer* (2015)
5) *Breaking Bad*
6) Elisabeth Moss
7) Afghan
8) *Life in Pieces* – debuted 2015
9) *Fresh Off the Boat* – debuted 2015
10) *The Originals* (2013-2018)

Quiz 5

1) What series stars Jason Bateman as Marty Byrde, a Chicago financial advisor who serves as a money launderer for a Mexican drug cartel, who must move his family to the lake region of Missouri when things go awry?

2) On the comedy *Silicon Valley*, Richard Hendricks, a Silicon Valley engineer, is trying to build his own company; what is the name of his company?

3) On *Supergirl*, what is the relationship between Supergirl and Superman?

4) What superhero series had a lead character who gained super strength and unbreakable skin from an experiment gone wrong?

5) What Oscar winner played Dr. Robert Ford, the creator of the theme park, on *Westworld*?

6) What science fiction series explores what it would be like if the Allies lost WWII, and Japan and Germany ruled the United States?

7) Who is the host of the documentary series featuring stories from former members of the Church of Scientology?

8) Who is the creator and star of the comedy *Master of None* about the life of a young actor in New York?

9) What drama is about politics in New York high finance and features U.S. Attorney Chuck Rhoades and hedge fund king Bobby Axelrod?

10) What series was a contemporary prequel to the movie *Psycho*?

Quiz 5 Answers

1) *Ozark* – debuted 2017
2) Pied Piper
3) Cousins
4) *Luke Cage* (2016–2018)
5) Anthony Hopkins
6) *The Man in the High Castle* – debuted 2015
7) Leah Remini – *Leah Remini: Scientology and the Aftermath*
8) Aziz Ansari
9) *Billions* – debuted 2016
10) *Bates Motel* (2013–2017)

Quiz 6

1) What comedy stars Ashton Kutcher, Debra Winger, and Sam Elliott?

2) On *Game of Thrones*, the seven kingdoms are part of what continent?

3) On *Longmire*, Walt Longmire was the dedicated sheriff of Absaroka County who is dealing with the death of his wife; what state was the show set in?

4) What comedy drama features a 1950s housewife who decides to become a stand-up comic?

5) Who plays Joyce Byers, the mother of the missing boy, on *Stranger Things*?

6) Who played the young rising country music star Juliette Barnes on *Nashville*?

7) On *Supergirl*, what is the name of Supergirl's alter ego?

8) On *Vikings*, what is the name of the settlement where the central

characters live?

9) What series is an American version of the 2010 Australian movie of the same name about a crime family and starred Jacki Weaver, Guy Pearce, Joel Edgerton and Ben Mendelsohn?

10) What anthology series explores how modern technologies can backfire and be used against their makers?

Quiz 6 Answers

1) *The Ranch* – debuted 2016
2) Westeros
3) Wyoming
4) *The Marvelous Mrs. Maisel* – debuted 2017
5) Winona Ryder
6) Hayden Panettiere
7) Kara Danvers
8) Kattegat
9) *Animal Kingdom* – debuted 2016
10) *Black Mirror* – debuted 2011

Quiz 7

1) What town was the setting for the fairy tale fantasy *Once Upon a Time*?
2) Before he was known as Saul Goodman what is the title character's name in *Better Call Saul*?
3) What series centers on a young Catholic woman who discovers that she was accidentally artificially inseminated?
4) Who plays bipolar CIA officer Carrie Mathison in the drama *Homeland*?
5) Who plays President Conrad Dalton on the political drama *Madam Secretary*?
6) What *Game of Thrones* actor has been nominated seven consecutive times for Best Supporting Actor in a Drama Series?
7) What is the name of the sporting goods store where Tim Allen's character works on *Last Man Standing*?
8) In what city was the fantasy drama *Grimm* set?
9) What character does Peter Dinklage play on *Game of Thrones*?
10) On *Designated Survivor*, what cabinet position did Tom Kirkman hold prior to being the designated survivor and becoming president?

Quiz 7 Answers

1) Storybrooke, Maine
2) Jimmy McGill
3) *Jane the Virgin* – debuted 2014
4) Claire Danes
5) Keith Carradine
6) Peter Dinklage
7) Outdoor Man
8) Portland, Oregon
9) Tyrion Lannister
10) Secretary of Housing and Urban Development

Quiz 8

1) In what century is the science fiction comedy *The Orville* set?
2) What mystery series had the tagline "All's fair in love and cold war"?
3) On *Empire*, Terrence Howard plays Lucious Lyon who must decide which of his sons will take over his company after he dies; what terminal illness does he have?
4) Who plays single mom Christy who is taking care of her two children and maintaining her sobriety while dealing with her recovering alcoholic mother on the sitcom *Mom*?
5) What comedy series presents historical reenactments as told by inebriated storytellers?
6) On *The Walking Dead*, what is the name of the deputy sheriff who wakes from a coma to learn the world is in ruins after a zombie apocalypse?
7) What Oscar winner plays the title role in the sitcom *Mom*?
8) What series featured a former superhero who is working as a New York City private investigator?
9) What crime drama anthology is inspired by a film by the Coen brothers who also serve as executive producers on the series?
10) Who played the title role of British murder detective John Luther who is brilliant but also obsessive and sometimes violent on *Luther*?

Quiz 8 Answers

1) 25th century
2) *The Americans* (2013-2018)

3) ALS
4) Anna Faris
5) *Drunk History* – debuted 2013
6) Rick Grimes
7) Allison Janney
8) *Jessica Jones* (2015–2019)
9) *Fargo* – debuted 2014
10) Idris Elba

Quiz 9

1) The original heir to *Downton Abbey* was killed in an accident making distant cousin Matthew Crawley the next in line to inherit the estate; how did the original heir die?
2) The sitcom *The Goldbergs* is set in the suburbs of what city?
3) What series was loosely based on a Stephen King story and had a female FBI agent dealing with the strange happenings in a small Maine coastal town?
4) Who plays Teresa Mendoza who flees Mexico to Dallas after her drug-dealing boyfriend is murdered on *Queen of the South*?
5) What sitcom features a real-life father, son, and daughter, and the father and son are also the show's creators?
6) What star of one of the favorite family dramas of the 1970s played Frank Gaad, a supervisor in the FBI counter-intelligence department, who was dedicated to identifying the Soviet spies on *The Americans*?
7) What science fiction mystery series was set in eight different countries around the world?
8) What action adventure reboot has the central character Angus who works for the Department of External Services (DXS), a clandestine U.S. government organization?
9) What superhero series title character was named Matt Murdock?
10) What Oscar winner plays Elliot Alderson on the thriller *Mr. Robot*?

Quiz 9 Answers

1) Aboard the *Titanic*
2) Philadelphia
3) *Haven* (2010–2015)
4) Alice Braga
5) *Schitt's Creek* – Eugene Levy and his real-life son Dan Levy are the

show's creators; Sarah Levy who is Eugene's daughter and Dan's sister also appears on the series.

6) Richard Thomas – John Boy of *The Waltons*
7) *Sense8* (2015–2018) – It told the story of eight people around the world who are suddenly linked mentally.
8) *MacGyver* – debuted 2016
9) *Daredevil* (2015–2018)
10) Rami Malek

Quiz 10

1) What British series centers on DCI Stanhope and her team who solve murder mysteries in the Northumberland area?
2) The early career of Dr. Phil McGraw of the *Dr. Phil* talk show inspired what crime drama series?
3) On *Revenge*, a young woman sets out to get revenge on the wealthy people who destroyed her father's life; where was the series set?
4) Who stars as the host of the reboot of the science show *Cosmos*?
5) What comedy drama starred Craig T. Nelson, Bonnie Bedelia, Ray Romano, Monica Potter, Dax Shepard, Lauren Graham, and Peter Krause?
6) Who plays the brilliant criminal defense professor Annalise Keating on *How to Get Away with Murder*?
7) Who plays Los Angeles area college professor Mort Pfefferman who decides to transition from being a male to a female on the comedy *Transparent*?
8) What former movie Superman plays the part of The Atom on *Arrow*?
9) What was the name of the character played by two-time Oscar winner Maggie Smith on *Downton Abbey*?
10) Who plays President Tom Kirkman on the political drama *Designated Survivor*?

Quiz 10 Answers

1) *Vera* – debuted 2011
2) *Bull* – McGraw earned his PhD in psychology from the University of North Texas in 1979 and founded Courtroom Sciences, Inc., a trial sciences firm, in 1980.
3) Hamptons, New York
4) Neil deGrasse Tyson

5) *Parenthood* (2010–2015)
6) Viola Davis
7) Jeffrey Tambor
8) Brandon Routh – He starred as Superman in *Superman Returns* (2006).
9) Violet Crawley – Dowager Countess of Grantham
10) Kiefer Sutherland

Quiz 11

1) *House of Cards* was an Americanized version of what British show?
2) On the sketch comedy show *Key and Peele*, what are the full names of the stars?
3) What is the real name of The Arrow on *Arrow*?
4) What two 2010s series reboots have multiple character crossovers?
5) What medical drama features Dr. Max Goodwin who wants to change the system as the new medical director at America's oldest public hospital?
6) What is the name of the family on the sitcom *Last Man Standing*?
7) What horror mystery series was set in the Norwegian arctic and was filmed in Iceland?
8) What science fiction series is based on a 1973 Michael Crichton film of the same name?
9) Who plays Captain Ray Holt, the head of the precinct, on *Brooklyn Nine-Nine*?
10) What series created by and starring Donald Glover centers on Earn and his cousin Alfred trying to make their way up in the world through rap?

Quiz 11 Answers

1) *House of Cards* – It aired on the BBC in 1990 and was based on a novel by Michael Dobbs who was a Chief of Staff and Deputy Chairman of the British Conservative Party under Prime Ministers Margaret Thatcher and John Major.
2) Keegan-Michael Key and Jordan Peele
3) Oliver Queen
4) *Hawaii 5-0* and Magnum P.I.
5) *New Amsterdam* – debuted 2018
6) Baxter
7) *Fortitude* (2015–2018)

8) *Westworld* – debuted 2016
9) Andre Braugher
10) *Atlanta* – debuted 2016

Quiz 12

1) Who played Captain Sharon Raydor of the Major Crimes Division of the LA Police Department on *Major Crimes*?
2) What historical drama is based on a series of Bernard Cornwell novels and tells the story of Uthred of Bebbanburg, an Anglo-Saxon raised by Danes?
3) What is the name of *The Walking Dead* spinoff that follows two families banding together to survive?
4) What science fiction drama has humans from hundreds of years in the future sending their consciousness back into people in the 21st century to try to change the path of humanity and avoid a terrible future?
5) What action series featured Marine veteran Frank Castle who becomes a vigilante after his family is murdered?
6) What crime series follows a fish out of water British police inspector working on the Caribbean island of Saint-Marie solving murders?
7) What mystery series set in the 1980s during the Cold War had two Russian agents posing as an average American married couple with two children?
8) On the sitcom *The Good Place*, who plays Michael, the architect of the good place?
9) What series centers on a young surgeon with autism and Savant syndrome who joins a prestigious hospital?
10) What son of a famous actor plays Danny Williams on *Hawaii Five-o*?

Quiz 12 Answers

1) Mary McDonnell
2) *The Last Kingdom* – debuted 2015
3) *Fear the Walking Dead* – debuted 2015
4) *Travelers* – debuted 2016
5) *The Punisher* (2017–2019)
6) *Death in Paradise* – debuted 2010
7) *The Americans* (2013–2018)
8) Ted Danson

9) *The Good Doctor* – debuted 2017
10) Scott Caan – son of James Caan

Quiz 13

1) On *Vikings*, what is the name of the central Viking warrior and farmer who sets out to explore and raid distant lands to the west?
2) Who stars in the title role on the series *Sherlock*?
3) What drama is based on the Israeli series *Prisoners of War* (2009)?
4) Who plays Dr. Watson on *Elementary*?
5) What is the name of the central family on the sitcom *Black-ish*?
6) On the superhero series *Daredevil*, what was the title character's daytime occupation?
7) What crime drama is set in the late 1970s with two FBI agents interviewing serial killers to solve cases and is based on the true experiences of FBI agent John Douglas who pioneered psychological profiling?
8) What series was a spinoff from a series of movies starring Noah Wyle?
9) What is the first name of the missing boy on *Stranger Things*?
10) On *Young Sheldon*, what is the explanation for why Sheldon doesn't have a Texas accent?

Quiz 13 Answers

1) Ragnar Lothbrok
2) Benedict Cumberbatch
3) *Homeland* – debuted 2011
4) Lucy Liu
5) Johnson
6) Lawyer
7) *Mindhunter* – debuted 2017
8) *The Librarians* (2014–2018)
9) Will
10) He switched his accent because people with Texas accents don't win Nobel prizes.

Quiz 14

1) What series centers on a set of triplets and their parents at different points in time?

2) On *Person of Interest*, an artificial intelligence identifies people who will be involved in a future violent crime; how are these people identified to the team?

3) Who plays the title role on the crime drama *Ray Donovan*?

4) What comedy featured a woman rescued from a doomsday cult in an underground bunker where she lived for fifteen years who moves to New York City to have a normal life?

5) What is the name of the hospital at the center of *Chicago Med*?

6) On the sitcom *Schitt's Creek*, how did Johnny Rose, played by Eugene Levy, make his money before losing it all?

7) What comedy series is based on the Venezuelan telenovela *Juana la Virgen*?

8) What anthology series features Kathy Bates, Jessica Lange, and Angela Bassett?

9) What is the name of the music company the main characters are battling for control of on *Empire*?

10) What Oscar winner plays the title character's ex-convict father on *Ray Donovan*?

Quiz 14 Answers

1) *This Is Us* – debuted 2016
2) Social security number
3) Liev Schreiber
4) *Unbreakable Kimmy Schmidt* (2015-2019)
5) Gaffney Chicago Medical Center
6) Video stores
7) *Jane the Virgin* – debuted 2014
8) *American Horror Story* – debuted 2011
9) Empire Entertainment
10) Jon Voight

Quiz 15

1) What science fiction author wrote the 1962 book of the same name that *The Man in the High Castle* is based on?

2) What HBO crime drama is an anthology series with a different cast and self-contained storyline each season focusing on police investigations?

3) What series set in the 1980s depicted an insider's view of the personal computing boom?

4) In *Outlander*, Claire Randall, a married combat nurse in 1945, is transported back in time to Scotland in what century?

5) Who stars in the title role in the sitcom *Man with a Plan*?

6) The series *Boardwalk Empire* centered on Enoch "Nucky" Thompson, an Atlantic City, New Jersey politician; what historical time period was it set in?

7) The series *GLOW* is set in the 1980s and features women performing in what activity?

8) What series has the tagline "The world's favorite detective has emerged from the fog"?

9) What is the name of James Spader's criminal mastermind character on *The Blacklist*?

10) The series *Downton Abbey* was inspired by what 2001 movie that was written by the series creator and writer Julian Fellowes?

Quiz 15 Answers

1) Philip K. Dick
2) *True Detective* - debuted 2014
3) *Halt and Catch Fire* (2014-2017)
4) 18th century - 1743 initially
5) Matt LeBlanc
6) 1920s Prohibition era
7) Professional wrestling
8) *Sherlock* - debuted 2010
9) Raymond Reddington
10) *Gosford Park* - Maggie Smith, Jeremy Swift, and Richard E. Grant appeared in both the movie and the series and Smith and Swift have similar roles in both.

Quiz 16

1) Who played the American mother Cora Crawley on *Downton Abbey*?

2) What series is based on a book of the same name and centers on a public relations executive who is sentenced to a minimum-security women's prison in Connecticut?

3) What series is set 97 years after a nuclear war with a group of juvenile delinquents being sent back to Earth in hopes of re-populating the planet?

4) What drama features teenager Clay Jensen as he tries to uncover the reason behind his classmate's suicide?

5) What is the name of the captain played by Seth MacFarlane on *The Orville*?

6) What series features an Irish American family with an alcoholic father and an eldest daughter who takes on the role of the parent to her five brothers on the South Side of Chicago?

7) What was the name of Kerry Washington's former White House staffer and professional fixer character on *Scandal*?

8) What animated comedy features Bob Belcher and his wife and three children trying to run a restaurant?

9) What character did Luke Perry play on *Riverdale*?

10) What is the name of Julia Louis-Dreyfus' character on *Veep*?

Quiz 16 Answers

1) Elizabeth McGovern
2) *Orange Is the New Black* – debuted 2013
3) *The 100* – debuted 2014
4) *13 Reasons Why* – debuted 2017
5) Ed Mercer
6) *Shameless* – debuted 2011
7) Olivia Pope
8) *Bob's Burgers* – debuted 2011
9) Fred Andrews
10) Selina Meyer

Quiz 17

1) Who plays the title role on *Better Call Saul*?

2) On *Gotham*, the character of Edward Nygma is better known as who?

3) What actor plays a White House staffer on *Designated Survivor* and worked as a White House staffer in their real life?

4) What animated comedy series features the adventures of a genius alcoholic scientist, with his not so smart grandson?

5) Who plays the father, Abe Weissman, on *The Marvelous Mrs. Maisel*?

6) What action adventure followed Captain Flint and his pirates twenty years prior to Robert Louis Stevenson's *Treasure Island*?

7) What are the unusually large and intelligent species of wolves called on *Game of Thrones*?

8) What series features a police detective in an asteroid belt who is part of a group that discovers a conspiracy that threatens the

Earth's colony?

9) For what series did Jeff Daniels win the Outstanding Lead Actor in a Drama Series Emmy?

10) In *House of Cards*, what state did Francis Underwood grow up in and represent in the U.S. House of Representatives?

Quiz 17 Answers

1) Bob Odenkirk
2) Riddler
3) Kal Penn – He was Associate Director of the Obama administration's White House Office of Public Engagement.
4) *Rick and Morty* – debuted 2013
5) Tony Shalhoub
6) *Black Sails* (2014–2017)
7) Direwolves
8) *The Expanse* – debuted 2015
9) *The Newsroom* (2012–2014)
10) South Carolina

Quiz 18

1) *Major Crimes* was a spinoff of what series?
2) What historical series was inspired by the leader of a slave uprising against the Roman Republic?
3) Who plays the title role in *The Man in the High Castle*?
4) What are the names of the three Goldberg children on *The Goldbergs*?
5) Who provides the voice for the title character on the animated comedy series *BoJack Horseman*?
6) The sitcom *Speechless* focuses on the family of a special-needs teen; what does the teen suffer from?
7) Who plays Pops, the grandfather, on the sitcom *Black-ish*?
8) Who played ex-CIA agent John Reese on *Person of Interest*?
9) Who plays the alcoholic father Frank Gallagher on *Shameless*?
10) On *Game of Thrones*, what is the capital of the Seven Kingdoms?

Quiz 18 Answers

1) *The Closer*
2) *Spartacus* (2010–2013)

3) Stephen Root
4) Erica, Barry, Adam
5) Will Arnett
6) Cerebral palsy
7) Laurence Fishburne
8) Jim Caviezel
9) William H. Macy
10) King's Landing

Quiz 19

1) On *Supergirl*, who stars as Supergirl's boss Cat Grant?
2) What series has the tagline "What if your future was the past?"
3) What sitcom has the tagline "Boldly running for president. Proudly standing for everything"?
4) Who played the title role on the sitcom *New Girl*?
5) What is Robert Crawley's title as the head of the family on *Downton Abbey*?
6) Who plays the title role in the drama *Madam Secretary*?
7) Who plays Smurf, the mother and leader of the crime family, on the crime drama *Animal Kingdom*?
8) What series is based on the *Archie Comics*?
9) What is the name of the magic school the central characters attend in *The Magicians*?
10) What drama series centered around the exploits of Colombian drug lord Pablo Escobar?

Quiz 19 Answers

1) Calista Flockhart
2) *Outlander* – debuted 2014
3) *Veep* – debuted 2012
4) Zooey Deschanel
5) Earl of Grantham
6) Tea Leoni
7) Ellen Barkin
8) *Riverdale* – debuted 2016
9) Brakebills
10) *Narcos* (2015–2017)

Quiz 20

1) What is the name of the big box store where the characters work on the sitcom *Superstore?*
2) In what city is the sitcom *Last Man Standing* set?
3) What fantasy drama centered on a homicide detective who discovers he is a descendant of hunters who fight supernatural forces?
4) What drama is set in a theocratic dictatorship in a dystopian future after a second American civil war?
5) What series features a group of friends motivated to living life to the fullest after the death of a close friend?
6) What sitcom is a spinoff continuation of *Full House?*
7) What big city crime drama follows both the uniformed police who patrol the beat and the Intelligence Unit, the team that combats the major offenses?
8) What is the real name of the title character on *The Flash?*
9) What series features a brilliant college dropout who finds himself working as a lawyer for one of New York City's top attorneys?
10) What animated comedy features a self-loathing alcoholic horse whose acting career peaked when he starred in a 1990s family sitcom called *Horsin' Around?*

Quiz 20 Answers

1) Cloud 9
2) Denver, Colorado
3) *Grimm* (2011–2017)
4) *The Handmaid's Tale* – debuted 2017
5) *A Million Little Things* – debuted 2018
6) *Fuller House* – debuted 2016
7) *Chicago P.D.* – debuted 2014
8) Barry Allen
9) *Suits* – debuted 2011
10) *BoJack Horseman* – debuted 2014

Made in the USA
Monee, IL
10 August 2020